UNS\
FOR FEMALES

CARRIE DUNN is a writer. Her recent books include *The Pride of the Lionesses*, nominated as Football Book of the Year in 2020, and *The Roar of the Lionesses: Women's Football in England*, one of the *Guardian*'s best sport books of 2016. She has covered the last three Women's World Cups for *The Times* and Eurosport and is a regular voice on BBC radio as well as *The Athletic* Women's Football podcast. She has a PhD in sport sociology, and her particular research specialism is women's experience of sport. Her own footballing career began – and ended – with the Junior Hatters' supporters' club in her hometown of Luton.

She lives in the beautiful Snowdonia National Park with her actor husband and their rescue lurcher, Spring.

PRAISE FOR CARRIE DUNN

'Dunn's passion and erudition seeps through every syllable'
The Guardian

'Carrie's forensic research and depth of knowledge make her the perfect person to guide us through the constantly changing landscape of women's football'

Kelly Cates, TV presenter

'Carrie Dunn's razor-sharp way with words and clever analysis of women's football history are worth paying attention to. You can't keep her quiet . . . but then you'd never want her to stay silent for too long!'

Kait Borsay, *The Offside Rule* podcast

'Dunn's meticulous research and careful choice of words leaves the reader entertained and informed in equal measure'

Matt Davies-Adams, commentator and broadcaster

'One of the most talented and considered minds working in women's football today'

Carl Anka, *The Athletic*

'Crisp and humane writing. A book that is rooted in the joy and pain of sport'

By the Book Reviews on *The Roar of the Lionesses*

'Rivetingly insightful and beautifully researched'

Football writer Julie Welch on *The Roar of the Lionesses*

UNSUITABLE FOR FEMALES:

THE RISE OF THE LIONESSES
AND WOMEN'S FOOTBALL IN ENGLAND

CARRIE DUNN

This edition published in 2023 by

ARENA SPORT
An imprint of Birlinn Ltd
West Newington House
10 Newington Road
Edinburgh
EH9 1QS

www.birlinn.co.uk

ISBN 978 1 913759 09 4

British Library Cataloguing-in-Publication Date
A catalogue record for this book is available
on request from the British Library.

Designed and typeset by Biblichor Ltd, Edinburgh
Printed by Clays Ltd, Elcograf, S.p.A.

To Henry and Emilia

CONTENTS

THE BEGINNING

THIS IS THE BOOK PEOPLE keep asking me to write.

After covering the Women's World Cup in 2015, I wrote *The Roar of the Lionesses*, following a season in the life of women's football in England. Four years later, I wrote the sequel, *The Pride of the Lionesses*, exploring what – if anything – had changed.

With both books, I stressed that I wanted to give a snapshot of life at all levels of the game. I wasn't going to just focus on the England team or the superstars of the Women's Super League. I wanted to tell the stories of the women all the way down the pyramid: their daily routines, their sacrifices, their love of football.

I tried to give a sense of the vast history of women's football as well. The late Sylvia Gore, ambassador for Manchester City, spoke to me for *Roar*; Gillian Coultard, long-time England captain, wrote the foreword. Two legendary goalkeepers played a big part in *Pride*, with Rachel Brown-Finnis writing the foreword and her predecessor between the England sticks, Pauline Cope, sharing her memories of her playing and coaching career.

But there are so many more stories to be told, reaching back over more than a century. Decades of football history have been obscured by record-keeping so limited or non-existent that great footballing careers have simply disappeared from view. Understandably, governing bodies and players prefer to focus on the here and now, pointing to current achievements rather than looking back at the challenges that were faced by previous generations.

I argue that it is crucial to know and understand the past. It's a truism that those who forget history are doomed to repeat it. However, it is also true that to remember the women footballers who blazed their own trails in their own ways is to shine a different light on today's game; it shows how complex and storied women's football is – and always has been. Scratch the surface, and uncover a fascinating tangle of lives.

ONE

THE RINGLEADER

IT'S A GLORIOUS NAME – NETTIE Honeyball.

She is the woman who led the British Ladies in their famous fixtures at the end of the 19th century.

There is just one problem, though. Nettie Honeyball never existed – no matter what variant spelling you try, there are no records of such a person.

The 19th century was a time of social change, particularly when it came to sport. But it was a very male, macho sporting sphere, and there was an idea that physical strength, religious conviction and one's ability to take on power and be a successful, strong leader were all interlinked. It all stemmed from the public school system – where boys were encouraged to take up a sport to make them stronger and more manly, suitably equipped to take up a role in governing the expanding British Empire.

Organised football – in a format a modern-day spectator would recognise – stems back to 1863, when the Football Association was formed. The founder of Barnes FC, Ebenezer Morley, had suggested to the press that there should be a way to establish the rules for football, just as the Marylebone Cricket Club (better known as the MCC) had done for cricket. In a meeting at the Freemasons' Tavern in Great Queen Street, captains, secretaries and creators of football clubs in the London and South East area formed their association with the intent to regulate the game – rather than playing matches by their own rules, which might vary by region or by school background, as had happened previously.

Sheffield FC has a claim to creating the first-ever set of rules for football, with founders Nathaniel Creswick and William Prest drawing up their own code – known as the Sheffield Rules – in October 1858, publishing them the following year. Even though rules were available, that did not mean every club adopted them. Sheffield FC became members of the Football Association in 1863, but still used their own rules – and occasionally the quirky rules of opponents, with their first fixture outside Sheffield coming in 1865 against Nottingham. It was not an 11-a-side encounter, though, as might have been expected; rather, there were 18 players on each side.

What was needed was more consistency, and a countrywide approach for competition. To that end, the FA Cup – or the Football Association Challenge Cup – was created in 1871, with all the member clubs invited to compete in a national knock-out tournament. Then the Football League was founded in 1888 when Aston Villa's William McGregor came up with the idea of regular fixtures for clubs, rather than one-off matches or challenges. The FA was still in charge, but the League operated within it. Though there continued to be disagreements about whether football should be an amateur sport or a professional one, a supposed 'gentlemen's game' or one that paid men for their hard labour on the pitch – a schism that split largely along the north–south divide – the structure of football by the turn of the century would be easily identifiable to today's fan.

Women's roles in the leisure sphere generally and football particularly were not part of any public discussion, and nor were they broadly encouraged to take up sport. But they were certainly both playing and watching it. Reporter Charles Edwardes noted in 1892 that it was not just working-class men who had 'football fever' and were attending matches, but many women as well, and he expressed surprise that 'the fair sex' were prepared to stand on the terraces. Before the Football League began in 1888, Preston North End were forced to withdraw their offer of free entry to ladies when 2,000 women turned up at the ground.

Middle-class girls were starting to play competitive team sports at school and at university – when they were allowed to attend, of course. Most often they were playing hockey, cricket or croquet, and sometimes they got to play individual sports (in 1884, the ladies' singles competition at Wimbledon began). But these were all somewhat in accordance with the stereotypical ideas of what kind of pastimes ladies ought to engage in. These were sports with no contact, and which allowed the participants to play wearing appropriate clothing – that is, long skirts. Football, however, was not judged to be appropriate. Although football for men was established, it was riven with those class divisions that were dogging the new Football Association and then the Football League, who suffered the same problems as cricket had, with working-class men earning money from their skills and the amateur 'gentlemen' tending to look down on them.

Nonetheless, some women broke free from expectations. It is thought that at least 150 'ladies' teams' were playing regularly in the first two decades of the 20th century, following in the footsteps of the Victorian women and girls who were enjoying less structured competition. In 1888, there was a match in Inverness between a team of married women and a team of single women, long believed to be the first match outside an educational setting, but historians now believe that the first home international took place seven years prior, on 9 May 1881, when teams playing under the names of 'England' and 'Scotland' faced off at Easter Road, Edinburgh, resulting in a 3–0 triumph for the Scots.

In 1894, the British Ladies' Football Club was established, with Honeyball listed as its secretary. Clearly a woman of drive and spirit, Honeyball placed advertisements in periodicals for other women interested in football, and created her club comprising players, administrators and supporters. They trained in Nightingale Lane, in North London, and according to the generally accepted histories even managed to secure coaching from a leading male player of the time: John William (Bill) Julian, the Tottenham Hotspur centre-half. Honeyball organised the now-famous match between the North and the South at Crouch End the year after, which attracted more than 10,000 fans. It also attracted plenty of media coverage, with the *Manchester Guardian*'s report sidetracked by the kits worn by the players: the North team wore 'red blouses with white yokes, and full black knickerbockers fastened below the knee, black stockings, red berretta caps, brown leather boots and leg pads' while the South wore 'blouses of light and dark blue in large squares, and blue caps'. The report added that some players also donned 'a short skirt above the knickerbockers, but this rather distracted from the good appearances of the dress, as the skirts flapped about in the wind and rendered movement less graceful.'

The *Guardian* surmised that the crowds had been drawn by the novelty factor, but reassured any women reading that they should not be put off by the inevitable lack of public interest in their sporting exploits and that they should continue to play for their own health and recreation. Despite that rather downbeat conclusion, the success of that North v. South match led to a UK tour sponsored by the British Ladies' club president Lady Florence Dixie.

The British Ladies' subsequent fixtures were relatively limited yet dramatic, with men drafted in on at least one occasion after players failed to show up for a fixture. There was also a messy misunderstanding in April 1895, when the British Ladies were supposed to be playing at the Royal Ordnance FC, in Maze Hill, South East London, but a telegram sent in the name of Nettie Honeyball cancelled the exhibition shortly after the scheduled kick-off time. With the FA Council starting to notice that the women's matches were attracting interest, they began informing clubs that 'lady footballers' should not be playing on their grounds. The Maze Hill fiasco also seemed to have triggered a schism in the club. Two separate teams were in operation from 1895 onwards, both calling themselves the 'Original Lady Footballers', and Honeyball disappeared from the teamsheets. It is possible that she might have taken on the name 'Nellie Hudson' instead, which appears frequently in the line-ups for one of the teams, but this is mere conjecture.

One of the biggest problems with tracing women's football history is the lack of records – and the earliest footballers added a twist to that issue by adopting pseudonyms for their sporting careers. Perhaps because football was still thought to be unbecoming for women to play (particularly bearing in mind they were out in public in relatively few clothes – a full-skirted dress, the usual attire for a woman, was certainly not conducive to playing football, and thus Honeyball and Dixie had encouraged their original crop of players to wear kit similar to those worn by male players of the time), perhaps because their families did not want their names attached to such controversy, or perhaps just for fun, the earliest female footballers were happy to take on stage names for their performances on the pitch.

So who was Nettie Honeyball, and did any of the British Ladies play under their own names?

There is a photo of a woman purported to be 'Honeyball' in the *Sketch* magazine from February 1895. She appears to be aged between 25 and 30, she is moderately tall and of sturdy build – indeed, she told the newspapers that she weighed over 11 stone. There is no other indication in the photograph as to who she might be, but in the article accompanying that photograph, the reader is given a strong sense of her personality. Honeyball is quoted as saying: 'There is nothing of the farcical nature about the British Ladies' Football Club. I founded the association late last year, with the fixed resolve of proving to the world that women are not the "ornamental and useless" creatures men have pictured. I must confess, my convictions on all matters, where the sexes are so widely divided, are all on the side of emancipation and I look forward to the time when ladies may sit in Parliament and have a voice in the direction of affairs, especially those which concern them most.'

Even the contemporary reports of the time could not agree on what they knew about her, but they tended to call her either 'Nettie Honeyball' or 'Nettie J. Honeyball'. One historian, James Lee, suggested that Nettie Honeyball could actually have been 'Nellie', born on 28 August 1873 in Pimlico, London; some of the press reports gave the variant first name, which could be accurate or of course a typographical error.

Some stories stated that she had a brother who travelled with the team and carried out some managerial duties; the *Sporting Man* newspaper interviewed this man in 1895 as part of their coverage of an exhibition match at St James' Park, Newcastle-upon-Tyne. Assuming that 'Honeyball' was a pseudonym and Lee was mistaken, the one piece of information that may give a clue as to who she might have been is her address, with some newspapers saying that she hailed from 27 Weston Park, in Crouch End, North London. That address was the home of Arthur Tilbury Smith and his family – including his son, Alfred Hewitt Smith, who was said by the *Kentish Gazette* to be the British Ladies' manager. In 1895, Miss Jessie Allen wrote to the *Manchester Courier* on the subject of women's football, describing herself as the secretary of the British Ladies, and giving her address as Weston Park, Crouch End. 'Miss Allen' was the maiden name of Mrs Jessie Mary Ann Smith. She was married to Frederick, the eldest son of Arthur Tilbury Smith

and Mary Watford, and thus she was sister-in-law to Alfred
Hewitt Smith. The jigsaw pieces do indicate that she may well
have been the original player to adopt the name 'Nettie
Honeyball'. If Jessie Smith née Allen was indeed Nettie Honeyball, her use of the name was relatively short-lived. She stopped
using the pseudonym by the end of 1895, and began playing
and serving as secretary under her maiden name. The amateur
historian Patrick Brennan points to census records that suggest
that Jessie and Frederick Smith were living in West Ham at the
time of the 1901 census, but by 1911 she had been widowed
and, childless, was living back with her father in Stoke
Newington, North East London. Brennan's analysis of the
registry records shows that Jessie later moved to Leigh-on-Sea
in Essex, and died at University College Hospital in the centre
of London on 3 October 1922, aged 52.

Honeyball presented herself as a respectable upper-middle-
class woman, indicating that the rest of her players came from
similar backgrounds. She was quoted as telling the *Maidenhead
Advertiser* at the time: 'If I accepted all the girls from the masses
that made application to join us, why, our list would have been
filled long ago.' Of course, the choice of the word 'Ladies' in
the team name was also deliberate in its similar connotations –
suggesting that these players were not ruffians or ragamuffins,
but refined, elegant women.

This was, however, surely a ruse. The fact that the British
Ladies were attracting public attention, putting on a spectacle,
and keen to bring a paying crowd through the turnstiles aligned
them more with the scorned male professionals rather than
their gentlemanly amateur peers who would not have dreamt of
taking any money for their sporting prowess.

TWO

THE MYSTERY

IN 2018, THERE WAS A major event. Anna Kessel, the chair of campaigning and networking group Women in Football, had been leading a campaign to recognise women's achievements with blue plaques – traditionally given out to mark places of significant historical interest. She spearheaded an event at the Royal Society as part of Black History Month, entitled 'Celebrating Emma Clarke, Black Female Football Pioneer'.

And in 2019, there was a blue plaque unveiled at Campsbourne School, in Nightingale Lane, Hornsey, North London, to honour the pioneering British Ladies team, who toured the country and played on the site, the former ground of Crouch End FC. Once again, it singled out Emma Clarke on what would have been her 148th birthday, declaring her to be the first black woman to play football in Britain. Keen student of sporting history Stuart Gibbs had made the declaration after carrying out some research, suggesting that she was the 'coloured lady of Dutch build' referred to in a match report in the *Stirling Sentinel* chronicling the exploits of the team known as 'Mrs Graham's XI', one of the two offshoots of the original British Ladies side. The phrase 'Dutch build' meant 'hefty' or 'bulky' at the time, and was not just used to apply to people, but to anything of size. As for the 'coloured lady', identifying her was tricky. Initially she was thought to be the goalkeeper listed on the teamsheet as Carrie Boustead. Unsurprisingly, however, there turned out to be no such person in the records as Carrie Boustead, or Caroline Boustead, or any other variant of the spellings.

Mrs Graham, however, is now generally believed to be Helen Graham Matthews, a Scottish prototype feminist and suffrage campaigner who, like her counterparts around the UK, took plenty of liberties with the truth when speaking to the press. Formerly one of the British Ladies goalkeepers, Mrs Graham said that all her players were from the Lancashire area, which led Gibbs to track down an Emma Clarke of about the right age in Bootle, near Liverpool. That was the birthplace given for her at the Royal Society's event.

Then Gibbs uncovered a newspaper report in Belfast that listed more detail about each player, which indicated that Clarke was in fact from Plumstead, South London. Perhaps Mrs Graham had been liberal with the truth in order to appeal to a particular local audience, or perhaps she was deliberately obfuscating in order to hide her players' identities. Whatever the reasoning, the confusion between the two women identi-fied as 'Emma Clarke' has meant that her actual story has become muddled, with many different versions being told – and more than one of them made into theatre productions portraying different narratives.

The Emma Clarke of Plumstead had direct descendants, who have not yet gone on record to talk about their ancestor, but her sister Florence's family have been happy to talk. The story that was passed down to them indicates that there may have been some kind of scandal in the sisters' past; another researcher, Andy Mitchell, drew up a family tree tracking the sisters' heritage.

Mitchell says that their grandfather, a Royal Artillery cor-poral called Edmund Bogg, spent four years serving at the British fort in Galle, on the south coast of Ceylon, now known as Sri Lanka. He and his wife Ann had a daughter Caroline there in December 1841, and at the age of 22, Caroline married

John Clarke – the son of another Royal Artillery man – in Woolwich. Emma was born in 1871, and Florence in 1877.

Mitchell had initially wondered whether Caroline Bogg was the product of an extra-marital affair, and thus of mixed race, but the birth records give her parents as Edmund and Ann. As he points out, that does not necessarily prove anything; she could have been adopted by them, or passed off as a child of the married couple to avoid any further questions.

'I was able to put together the story of the real Emma Clarke born in Plumstead, and that in itself was kind of straightforward,' he said, admitting that the Emma Clarke from Bootle disappears from history after 1903. 'But then the big question, was she actually black? And that's where of course it gets quite interesting because there is a family myth, and this was totally unprompted by media stuff because the family had no idea that she was a famous footballer; nobody had ever raised it with them. It was one of the other descendants of Florence who said, "Yeah, my granny always said there was some sort of family secret about the Indian Raj." Well, that's interesting, but pinning it down is another matter entirely.

'So it remains a mystery as to whether she was actually black or . . . if there was some other family secret, or whether or not the whole thing is just a big misunderstanding.'

Mitchell stepped away from the entire story, explaining: 'The whole thing is incredibly difficult. Having dipped my toe in the arguments of Emma Clarke, I've taken a back seat. I thought I'm not going to get anywhere here; there's plenty of other people who are far more interested.'

Gibbs, however, has continued to work in an effort to uncover more of Clarke's story. He was the leading researcher supporting the campaign for the plaque to honour her, which was eventually put in place by community group Nubian Jak, and sponsored by Black History Walks.

However, not everyone is convinced that Clarke should have been recognised in that way – or indeed that much of her story is confirmed at all. Mitchell is one of those with significant doubts.

'There was this thing about having a plaque,' said Mitchell, 'and I said, "Well, you're really having a stab in the dark here, saying this is correct," but they were determined to go ahead, so I said, "Fine, I'm not going to endorse it and say this is wonderful."'

Professor Jean Williams, an expert in women's football history, also had major misgivings at the time, and said she felt there is currently a lack of evidence pointing to Clarke's black heritage; she felt uneasy about relying on conclusions drawn solely from a handful of black-and-white photographs from the end of the 19th century. When the Royal Society hosted the event celebrating the Emma Clarke from Bootle, Williams felt that the evidence was shaky.

When the Royal Society hosted the event celebrating the Emma Clarke from Bootle, Williams tried to convince those involved that the evidence was shaky. Apart from anything else, she pointed out that Emma Clarke who played for the British Ladies could not have been from Bootle, because all Nettie Honeyball's press interviews indicated that the matches were between North London and South London – not North of England and South of England, and not a national match. This is borne out by the initial teamsheets; if one accepts that Jessie Allen of Crouch End was using the name Nettie Honeyball, she is in the first-ever British Ladies line-up, representing the 'North'; Clarke, of Plumstead, is on the opposite side, the 'South'.

Williams also argued that Caroline Clarke, née Bogg, being born in Ceylon was no proof either way of any black or Asian heritage that would have been passed down to her daughter.

'Given the size of the British army and the British Empire at that time, lots of white British kids are going to be born in

Ceylon, so that's not that remarkable,' she said. 'If there was a family scandal [around the birth of Caroline] the parents certainly went on to have more children together so it didn't break the family up.

'As a historian, I think we're on very thin ground. [The campaigners] got family historians involved and they said, "Well, families all have secrets." Yeah, they do. But as far as we go, the genealogical evidence – because again both parents sign both sets of their [registry] certificates that I've seen – there is no evidence for any split or anything in the family. If you follow the paper trail there is no evidence.'

As for the newspaper reports, Williams suspected that the references to Emma Clarke's 'darkness' were descriptions of hair colour. 'I accept that she is described as a dark girl, and her sister is described as a fair girl – but my interpretation of that is to be their hair colour. Again, [that is] not that unusual because the women tend to be distinguished by their hair. The other thing is this "woman of Dutch build". Now, if you read any Charles Dickens or anything, somebody of Dutch build is substantially built, it is a kind of euphemism for generously proportioned – so you can have a Dutch side-board! It doesn't mean that she's even foreign. We know Nettie Honeyball was about ten and a half stone, which would have been relatively robust for a Victorian woman of the time. So I just take it that it is the journalist's sexist way of saying women who want to play football have to be pretty robust of build.'

Despite the doubts raised by some historians, the FA hail Clarke as 'Britain's first female BAME footballer', and in the media her name has been mentioned as one of the 'black pioneers of the women's game' – possibly even 'the first black female professional footballer', assuming she and her teammates did indeed get a small remittance for their efforts on behalf of the British Ladies. Her place in women's football history has been assured even without the conclusive photographic evidence or genetic proof that some historians are still searching for, and which would dismiss any doubts once and for all. Nettie Honeyball may have been a pseudonym and Emma Clarke a real person, but both have become significant parts of women's football tradition despite so little information about either of them. Of course, women's history in general has been neglected, not chronicled in the same way that men's stories might have been, and often tough to trace in public records because of the custom of women changing their surnames upon marriage. The struggles to track down women from the past are not unique to football historians. With a relative dearth of knowledge about the women whose football careers developed in parallel with the men's competitions in the late 19th and early 20th centuries, fables and legends have been created around mysterious, elusive figures.

THREE

THE MYTH

LILY PARR IS PERHAPS THE first genuine, established superstar of women's football. There is no question about her existence or her footballing career, which extended into the second half of the 20th century and as such was slightly better reported than her earlier years.

Her basic autobiographical facts are indisputable. She was born on 26 April 1905, to parents George and Sarah – their fourth child of seven. She grew up in St Helens, and the family were certainly short of money. She moved to Preston to look for work, and ended up with a job at the Dick, Kerr factory, which produced ammunition for the forces during the First World War.

Parr became part of their famous football team – the Dick, Kerr Ladies. The team had initially been set up after some of the factory girls joined in with the lads to have a kickabout during their breaks. After the men's recreational team had a poor run of results, the girls were teasing their colleagues, and it ended up with the boys throwing down a challenge to them, which was quickly accepted, and the two sides faced off in October 1917. The factory girls kept on with their newly formed team, and were soon approached by a local hospital who wanted them to help with fundraising efforts for wounded soldiers. Rather than staging a concert, the girls opted to put on a football match, and asked the neighbouring Arundel Coulthard Foundry to form the opposition. The Dick, Kerr squad was selected after trials of the factory's ladies' sports club, which had 200 members, and one of the company's draughtsmen Alfred Frankland took on the role of manager.

Wartime gave women a bit of leeway when it came to occupations and pastimes that had previously been the sole domain of men. Women were needed to do the jobs vacated by men who had joined the armed forces, and it seems to have been tacitly accepted that women were also going to do other typically 'male' things – like playing football. The authorities only permitted this during the war, though. The ban on women's football in England was notoriously rubber-stamped in 1921, but there had been plenty of indications that it was imminent in the decades before that. The FA Council had warned their clubs that they should not be allowing the ladies' teams to use their grounds as far back as the 1890s; and in 1902 they passed a motion forbidding all affiliated associations to give permission for their players to participate in matches against women. That was despite the huge amounts of money that women's football matches were raising for good causes – not just those involving Dick, Kerr Ladies. The years immediately after the First World War were ones of immense poverty around the country, including in its major cities; financial assistance from charitable organisations in lieu of the formalised social security safety nets was essential, and women's football was a massive part of that. A charity would ask two teams to play a fundraising match, the FA would be asked for permission to use a particular ground, and the club would work with the visiting ladies' teams to promote and put on the event. It was a system that seemed to work very well. The 1920 Boxing Day match between Dick, Kerr and St Helens is famous for its venue, Everton's Goodison Park, and its huge attendance of 53,000, with thousands turned away due to the stands already being at capacity, but it was also notable for the money made through gate receipts – over £3,000. Large amounts of money coming into the coffers was of interest to the FA, whose decision to ban women's football was thought to have been partly influenced by the suspicion that not all the cash raised reached the charities for which they were intended – and that some of the female players may have been paid to appear in matches.

Dick, Kerr's general manager Frankland tried to dismiss all these rumours, writing in the journal *Sports Pictures*: 'Those responsible for the charity must make all the arrangements themselves and accept all responsibility for payments made in connection with the match. All we have received wherever we played has been just our expenses, and [these] in no way include any pecuniary recompense for playing . . . Our sole ambition has been to help as much as we possibly could the numerous charities on whose behalf we have been asked to play. We have all given our services gladly and the girls have revelled in the football.'

Women's football was becoming hugely popular, evidently profitable and, ultimately, uncontrollable. In the summer of 1921, the FA gave permission for Dick, Kerr Ladies to play a South of England team on the home ground of Bristol City on the proviso that a full statement of accounts was shown to them immediately afterwards. A few months later, men's league clubs were instructed to seek permission from the FA before allowing women to play on the pitches, no matter what charity would benefit from a match being held, and that if permission were granted, the club itself had to take responsibility for the accounts. Clubs were punished if they did not obey this new rule, and it became obvious that there were some dissenters within the FA's membership – clubs, players and managers who were willing to continue to support women's football.

The FA cracked down hard. In December 1921, it issued its famous declaration:

Complaints having been made as to football being played by women, Council feel impelled to express their strong opinion that the game is quite unsuitable for females and should not be encouraged.

Complaints have also been made as to the conditions under which some of the matches have been arranged and played, and the appropriation of receipts to other than charitable objects. The Council are further of the opinion that an excessive proportion of the receipts are absorbed in expenses and an inadequate percentage devoted to charitable objects.

For these reasons the Council requests the Clubs belonging to the Association refuse the use of their grounds for such matches.

The careful use of the passive voice and the shocking allegations of financial impropriety go some way to obscuring the emphasis of the first sentence – the idea that football was unsuitable for women, full stop, harking back to those concerns over unladylike sporting activities more than three decades earlier. There was also an implication – indeed, an argument that was made explicit by some commentators – that it was unsuitable for women's bodies. For some critics, women footballers were not only risking injury during a match, they were risking long-term damage – possibly ruining their fertility and their chances of having a family later in life.

Such a proclamation could not wipe out women's football entirely. At that time, there were approximately 150 women's clubs in England, and they pulled together quickly to set up the English Ladies' Football Association. They brought in some governing principles as swiftly as possible – one of the most notable being that no woman could play for a team more than 20 miles from her home, meaning that the close-knit local ties of teams and communities were preserved and encouraged.

Some of the better-established teams had access to their own pitches and did not need to rely on the generosity and cooperation of men's clubs. Dick, Kerr Ladies, for example, had their own facilities at Ashton Park, but they were supported by the factory and company whose name they bore. Nor did the Dick, Kerr Ladies particularly see a need to be involved in a domestic league competition; their fame had spread abroad and they were invited to tour Europe, Canada and the United States. In 1926, the Dick, Kerr factory cut ties with its famous football team, which took on the name Preston Ladies instead, but to all intents and purposes it was the same side.

All in all, it was amazing that Lily Parr had such footballing longevity. Stunningly tall, and blessed with a magnificent head of jet-black hair, Lily Parr was an imposing figure to look at, and as a footballer she was a fearsome prospect too. She joined the Dick, Kerr side at the age of 14, in early 1920, having already spent time playing for St Helens, where she scored 43 goals in her first season. Even after the team were told to stop using the factory's name and called themselves Preston Ladies instead, Parr continued as a mainstay of the side, terrorising defences, marauding down the left wing. She played her last match in July 1951, gracing the pitch at Windsor Park in Belfast, as Preston and a representative French side toured the British Isles. By that time, Parr had moved into defence as a full-back, where she may well have played at the start of her career if some early reports with their graphics of tactical formations are to be trusted. There she impressed with her vision and calm control, and as a veteran and club loyalist she was even prepared to go in goal if required. Although no detailed records were kept, it is likely that she notched over 1,000 goals during her three-decade-long career with the club.

Like many of the other players, after she left her job at the Dick, Kerr factory, she became a nurse at the Whittington Hospital, a large psychiatric institution near Preston, and worked there until her retirement in the 1960s. She was diagnosed with breast cancer in her sixties, and underwent a double mastectomy, which prolonged her life by ten years. She died at home in Goosnargh on 24 May 1978, and her memorial can be found in her native St Helens.

So much is known about Parr primarily due to the work of Gail Newsham, a footballer herself in the 1970s, who took on the role of historian for Dick, Kerr Ladies, recording as best she could their half-century of almost secret, and almost entirely ignored, football matches. As a Preston girl herself, she had heard the oral tradition of the famous women's team, and in 1992 a local festival gave her the chance to bring former players together. She advertised in the local press, and began to talk to the women who had once worn Dick, Kerr's colours, quickly realising that if this part of history was not to be lost entirely, she would need to get everything recorded. She first published her book *In a League of Their Own!* in 1994 and updated it in several subsequent editions as she continued to uncover information, locating plenty of newspaper coverage of the team right up into the 1960s.

'It's not just a bunch of women having a kickabout for charity, it's something bigger than that, so I just thought to myself, somebody's got to do something before it's too late,' explained Newsham. 'I honestly believe if I hadn't done it then, we'd have lost such a lot. That was it for me. The more I found out, the more I wanted to know. I just couldn't believe the success and the size of the story and everything. It's taken over my life, not just in researching.

'To me, I still think of them as the young lasses that they were – I feel like we're mates. I know you might think I'm loopy, but I don't care – I honestly believe that they chose me to tell this story, because I always felt somebody were guiding me. I'd had no experience. I left school at 15, because you did in those days, you didn't go to university or owt, so I haven't got any qualifications to speak of. It just all fell together, and that's how it is all the time with this story.'

She is also probably the foremost authority on Parr, having spoken to so many of her team-mates.

Parr's early life is well chronicled by Newsham, who interviewed Alice Norris – also a Dick, Kerr player and worker, and with whose family Parr lodged. Norris described Parr as a loner, and could not recall her ever talking about her family. But she – as well as other players – also described a woman with a magnificently droll sense of humour, with Joan Whalley saying, 'You would have died laughing at her.' Whalley also told Newsham about Parr's light-fingered habits, taking souvenirs from some of their games, most usually an autographed match ball, particularly if it bore the signature of a local celebrity who had been the day's special guest.

Newsham writes of an incident where Parr was challenged before a match at Chorley in Lancashire by a professional male goalkeeper, who told her, 'You might look good kicking in against other women, but you'd never score a goal against me.' The tale goes that Parr proceeded to hammer home a shot that he attempted to stop, but the sheer power of it broke his arm, much to her amusement and satisfaction.

Such is the power of Parr's story – the working-class girl with a magical gift for football – there has been plenty of interest in her in more recent years. And this boom has also led to problems. Some of the little fables that are told about Parr are perhaps exaggerations, and Newsham was aware of that.

'She's just been made into something that never existed,' she said. 'She was just an ordinary lass, a good player with a powerful shot in a very good team, and there were better players than her; it's just that she played longer than anybody else.'

'It's like most great footballers,' said Jean Williams. 'People will claim to have had a drink with George Best. You've even got Norman Mailer in *The Fight*, writing about going for a morning jog with Muhammad Ali, after pulling an all-nighter and he is in as good a shape as Ali. Our heroes, we like to invest in them, we like to magnify.'

However, some of the other stories have more than a grain of truth. 'There is lots of evidence that she was really quite naughty!' laughed Williams. 'I did interview some of the players. They did enjoy themselves and they had a lovely time.'

But the caricature of the chain-smoking, coarse, rude, wild girl is, according to Williams, unfair. 'When I've seen Lily Parr [in photographs] at the various events she's in a posh frock. She looks as good in a posh frock and a little cloche hat as she leaves for France as anybody else. I think that coarseness may have been overplayed. And, of course, people are complicated so maybe she did like a fag but was it 40 a day? I've never seen any evidence of that.'

More significantly, Parr's name has been attached to initiatives for lesbian, gay, bisexual and trans people, a move that shocked her family, who maintain that she would not have described herself in any of those terms. Well-intentioned people saw the story of a great footballer, of immense physical stature, unmarried, with close female friends and no known male partner, and adopted her as a trailblazer for their own causes – but Parr's life and home set-up were far from unusual at the time. Assuming her sexuality simply from her marital status would be an error.

'That is a backward reading of the situation,' said Williams. 'The situation was a million young men, mostly between the ages of 18 and 21, were killed in the Great War [between 1914 and 1918]. So, as a social historian, there were a lot of single women [of the same generation in the years afterwards].

'If you look at what hockey did, the hockey administrators actually formed links with the Empire, and Australia and New Zealand, and lots and lots of young women are encouraged to go to Australia and New Zealand at this time to try and get a husband, because [in those countries] there are loads of spare men. So it's all a bit kind of functional and not what would be called romantic. I think people had to do whatever they could.'

Williams agreed that the evidence from the time suggested that the women of Dick, Kerr Ladies were very close friends, and Lily Parr certainly shared her home with another woman.

'Is it for us to say what those friendships were in terms of relationships? I don't particularly think so. So, yes, Lily lived with another woman and [her nephew] assured me that they were no more than friends, and the family were very upset by the creation of an LGBT Cup in Lily's name. But that's all we've got to go on.

'Today, we wouldn't judge anybody else's relationship, would we? So that's where I am with that.'

Essentially, the figure of Lily Parr – the woman and the footballer – has become a myth. There are few people left who knew her personally, but there are plenty who know her now due to Gail Newsham's assiduous work finally being acknowledged. In 2021, the National Football Museum in Manchester added to the statue of Parr unveiled two years previously, and established a gallery to display her legacy. Perhaps fittingly for a woman whose life narrative has become such a mixture of fact and fable, the museum's artefacts combine historical documents and memorabilia along with artwork inspired by her stories.

The real question should be whether or not the mythical status of Parr really matters. Is it important that Parr and her career have been written about so much, and that she has been honoured by football historians in ways that her team-mates have not? Perhaps in the end Parr is a symbol for all the Dick, Kerr Ladies and those forgotten women who played football in the first half of the 20th century, just as Emma Clarke signifies the women from black and minority ethnic backgrounds who were playing football in England and have never had their names recorded, and Nettie Honeyball stands for all the early administrators who were working tirelessly to find opponents and venues for their teams.

'We've all been party to that mythmaking – and I think it's hugely problematic, actually,' said Williams. 'If you hang it all on Lily Parr and one personality you kind of make the others fade into the background.'

There are scores of other female footballers from the inter-war period whose stories are just as colourful and outrageous as the myths around Lily Parr, and Williams thought they were 'varnished over' in the rush to concentrate solely on the tall striker.

'I think it's because women's sport is talked about in terms of "she was the first" or "she was this" or "she was that",' said Williams. The narrow prism through which women's sport tends to be discussed in the 21st century is also applied to the footballers of a century ago, making for a less than broad and unsatisfyingly uncomprehensive history. 'We need to be sensitive to the way in which people were trying to live their lives. I think these very simple stories get picked up – Emma Clarke was the first, Lily Parr was this – they are simple stories that get picked up quite widely by journalists, and that just magnifies that.'

Stephen Bolton has become one of the foremost authorities on Lily Parr's later career almost by accident. He is the grandson of Lizzy Ashcroft, one of Parr's team-mates and colleagues at the Whittingham Hospital, and as such has a treasure trove of documents and memorabilia about their footballing achievements, some of which he presented to the National Football Museum to enable them to launch their Lily Parr Gallery. His collection includes a scroll sent to Ashcroft by the hospital thanking her for her decade of service between 1926 and 1936.

In his uncle's loft, Bolton found three suitcases full of his grandmother's sporting memorabilia, untouched in over three decades. In a moving aside in one of his own articles, he recalled seeing the first case full of photographs and noted that he was unable to even identify his own grandmother as the young footballer that she was, because at the time the family had only one photo of her, and their memories were all of her as an old lady.

Lizzy Ashcroft was three months older than Parr, born on 8 January 1905, to miner Ralph and his wife Mary – one of nine siblings – and also a St Helens girl. Both turned out for St Helens FC, although their spells there did not overlap, with Ashcroft first turning out for them in April 1921. She made her debut for St Helens against Stoke in front of 30,000 spectators at the famous St Andrew's, Birmingham City's ground. St Helens folded after the FA ban in 1921, but Ashcroft moved on to Dick, Kerr Ladies. Both spent most of their footballing careers with Dick, Kerr (or the Preston Ladies); Ashcroft signed for them in 1923 and retired in 1935. Interestingly, the photos Bolton had of the two of them together showed Parr and Ashcroft standing at about the same height. He knew that Ashcroft was around five feet eight inches in her young adulthood, which would make Parr around the same – still significantly tall for the era, but not the six feet her myth purported her to be.

Fascinatingly, he has revealed that their sporting skills stretched way beyond one sport. Ashcroft was the Dick, Kerr vice-captain for three years – Parr's deputy – and took over as skipper from 1935. Bolton's research suggests that when Ashcroft assumed the captaincy, Parr had stepped back from football in order to concentrate on some of the other sports at which she excelled.

Recruiting staff to work at the Whittingham, which was, after all, the county mental hospital, was difficult. There was a stigma attached to mental health conditions, and people working with patients would need to be physically strong. The tall, powerful, fit women of the Dick, Kerr Ladies were ideal recruits.

'To take on board all these superstar women who could cope with these very difficult patients was a no-brainer,' Bolton said. 'And of course, 1926, the country is still on its knees and then you have got all the strikes, the Depression into the late '20s through to the Wall Street Crash. There was very little high-profile women's football going on – it was a difficult time for everybody.'

For Bolton, the sporting facilities at the Whittingham Hospital enabled working-class women like Parr and Ashcroft – who began working there after the Dick, Kerr factory ended their association with the football team – to excel in arenas they might not have otherwise been able to access. That included a team in the Preston and District Women's Cricket League, which began in 1934, with several of the big local employers wanting to offer their female employees the same activities that they had long offered the men. One of Bolton's key assertions in his work has been that a job at Whittingham County Mental Hospital was only possible if an applicant was a good sportsperson or had some musical talent. Some of the newspaper records do seem to bear that out – with one season's star cricketer promptly turning out for the Whittingham side the year after.

In September 1938, the *Grantham Journal* reported on a civic reception for the Dick, Kerr Ladies and a fundraising football match for the local hospital. It also noted the coincidence 'that the Preston team should include five nurses', including Parr, all of whom worked at the Whittingham.

Newspaper records show that Parr was a very handy cricketer, coming third in the 1938 batting averages, her Dick, Kerr team-mate Joan Whalley proving nifty with the ball, and Ashcroft also playing in the Whittingham side. Parr also turned out for the Whittingham Ladies' Hockey team in the Lancashire Central Women's Hockey League, and Bolton thought that it could have been at this point that Ashcroft became Dick, Kerr captain. The *Lancashire Evening Post* ran a story in September 1937 with the line, 'Lily Parr – from football to hockey' – and Bolton was unable to uncover any records of Parr playing football in 1935 or 1936 after stepping down from serving as captain. Instead, she was playing plenty of hockey.

Lizzy Ashcroft's life away from the football pitch sheds additional light on some of the myths around Lily Parr. Bolton's collection of memorabilia also bears witness to Ashcroft's relationship with her colleague, friend and so-called soulmate Alice McGrath. The pair met before Ashcroft's marriage, and after the death of Ashcroft's husband – Bolton's grandfather – from pneumonia in 1949, McGrath helped to bring up the two Ashcroft boys, who unsurprisingly spent a lot of time on the Whittingham grounds.

Bolton shared Jean Williams' views that many working-class women – single or widowed – were sharing their homes and creating lives together, splitting the costs of bills and accommodation. He still refuted the idea that the word 'lesbian' or 'gay' could be applied to Ashcroft and McGrath, or any of the other women of that era who, without husbands for whatever reason, found comfort and support in their close female relationships. Anecdotally, he knew many women of his grandmother's age who shared a household with a female friend, and were known to the rest of the family as an 'auntie'.

'Modern historians are grappling with this, because they want to celebrate the independence that these individuals had, but the burden of modern labelling isn't helpful,' he said.

'I didn't know Lily Parr. I met Lily Parr. I was introduced to her briefly one day. I certainly knew my granny, and I certainly knew very well my other granny and her sisters, and they were all the same ilk. There were so many women living together. There were so many men that suffered because of the war. Accommodation was short, times were tight, life was about existing.'

Bolton said that several of the women would certainly have been same-sex attracted, because simple statistics would suggest that; but to apply the term 'lesbian' or 'gay' or 'queer' to any of them, reading their history from a modern standpoint, was inaccurate and unhelpful. For him, rather than co-opting Lily Parr as an LGBTQ icon based on limited evidence, her legacy should be remembered differently.

'She should be celebrated today just for being a tremendous sportswoman, being a very well-thought-of and caring nurse, and a loyal friend,' he suggested.

FOUR

THE PHOTOGRAPH

THERE IS ONE VERY FAMOUS image of Wendy Owen during her football career. Aged 18, and in the dressing room before England's first-ever official match, she is turned slightly away from the rest of her team-mates sitting on the benches alongside her, and angled towards a camera peering in at this historic moment. Her long blonde hair falls down either side of her face, and she is holding a make-up palette, her right hand raised towards her face, applying some eyeshadow.

It wasn't a true reflection of what Owen was like, but it was the kind of image the media wanted to portray in the early 1970s, when women's football began to be acknowledged, even if only the smallest bit.

The FA's official prohibition on women playing football on league grounds continued until 1971, but that made no difference to the female footballers who had carried on with their matches in the face of the ban over the course of 50 years. Dick, Kerr Ladies might have been the most famous of the clubs, but there were others scattered all over the country. Just as Dick, Kerr Ladies – and plenty more women's factory teams in the early part of the 20th century – had been formed initially by an enthusiastic group of workmates, many other women's teams coalesced around a place of employment between the World Wars and beyond. The women who worked at the famous Lyons tea rooms in London formed their own works club, putting out five separate teams, with training facilities provided for them at Sudbury, Middlesex. Bath Ladies were founded in 1920, independent of a workplace or educational establishment, and enjoyed plenty of support from their male counterparts in the town – with one of the Bath City AFC officials serving as their manager. Some cities even boasted more than one team – Plymouth, for example, where in the 1920s there were apparently two separate sides using the place name, The Plymouth and District Amateur Ladies Athletic and Football Club, and an older team who adjusted their name to become known as The Plymouth International Ladies FC. Indeed, the letters page of the *Western Morning News* at that time was often scattered with correspondence from representatives of the clubs as well as rivals. For example, in December 1921 one correspondent, signing themselves simply 'Spectator', praised what they described as 'the original Plymouth Ladies' Football Club', with a passing mention of 'the new club who played at Wearde Camp', calling their efforts 'pathetic'; and in April 1922 a Mabel Gilbert, evidently one of the players representing the team of Marazion in Cornwall, wrote to the same newspaper in April 1922 to complain about 'the Plymouth Ladies/Association Football and Athletic Club' passing themselves off as Cornish in an earlier exhibition match.

The creation of clubs was driven by the keenness of the players themselves, who wanted to spend their leisure time learning a new skill, indulging their passion for the sport. Of course, many of these teams were set up solely or primarily to play charity matches, particularly during and just after wartime, but there were also challenge matches, and everything at this point was reliant on networks of volunteers, often communicating by post. Women's football gradually became more independent, with players taking part for love of the game and for competition, not just to raise money. After the establishment of the English Ladies' Football Association, it was noticeable that the vast majority of affiliated teams were in the North West and Midlands, with a cluster of clubs in the South East and South West. Huge efforts were made to set up teams in the south of England, particularly in London, where clubs were struggling to find local opponents. Eventually leagues were organised to allow women to play in a more structured fashion – even if the FA did not like it.

The FA Council reiterated their ban on women's football in the decades to come, most notably in 1946. Geoffrey Green, who wrote a history of the FA in 1953, addressed women's football in a few brief lines as he dismissed it as a blight on the game, saying: 'There now remain a few subjects upon which the FA have taken a definite stand from the beginning and remained unwavering in their attitude towards them. Amongst these may be counted Women's Football, Greyhound Racing, Betting and Rough Play.'

Such superior pronouncements did not affect the dedication of those already playing. Dick, Kerr Ladies – or Preston Ladies as they were officially known – continued to recruit the best young female talent, attracted by the legendary tales that enveloped the club. In 1960, they signed up a promising 13-year-old from Chorley, Lancashire, named Sheila Porter.

'I used to go playing football in the recreation ground, took a ball and joined in with the boys there,' she remembered. 'In them days, ladies – girls – didn't play football. But I just loved it so much and the lads used to say, "Come on, Sheila, you can join in our team," which was good.'

The rest of the Preston squad were much older than Sheila, but nonetheless welcoming to a player they could see had plenty of potential. She made her debut for the famous old team in June 1961, and spent two years there before joining Fodens in nearby Sandbach in 1963.

The big difference between playing with the lads and with a women's team was, she thought, simple – women were more likely to pass you the ball. 'But it was the same sport, if you will,' she added quickly. 'Lasses played it just the same as the lads did, which was good – you didn't see them in them days, no, you only saw the boys' football.'

Wendy Owen's football fandom had begun as a small child, and her first real set of idols were all part of England's 1966 World Cup winning squad. As a 12-year-old, it made a massive impression on her.

'I remember after that World Cup I'd be out in the back garden, juggling, kicking the ball, and I can remember I would imagine I was Geoff Hurst or Martin Peters, so that was pretty influential,' she said. Her father took her to watch Fulham, and later she loved to watch Don Revie's successful Leeds United side. Like any child of that era, she was also hugely in awe of Manchester United's pin-up George Best.

'I remember so well him coming and playing against Fulham. We were behind the goal, and he was dribbling towards the Fulham goal – and then we had a big crush, because it was standing in those days, and the crowd started to crush down.

'All the kids got passed to the front, because we were in danger of getting crushed, and we were allowed to climb up the floodlight – you wouldn't be allowed to now.'

Unsurprisingly, she had no female role models, but as a keen and strong sportswoman, she got to try out all the activities she wanted, encouraged by her family. Owen's grammar school teachers were not entirely supportive of her interest in football; however, her natural athletic ability meant she also excelled at netball, representing Wales, the country of her father's birth. Owen's football career started in less auspicious surroundings as she asked her father to set up a football team she could play in via the Beaconsfield Youth Club. Even better than that, he became a leading light in the South Bucks Youth Clubs League, meaning the girls had other teams to play against. When she was banned from playing football alongside the boys in competitive matches due to the FA's regulations preventing mixed football after the age of 11, she was fortunate enough to find that she had a women's team very nearby.

A little further afield from her home county of Berkshire, Thame Ladies in Oxfordshire had had a similar start to life in 1969 as a youth club team for girls in the area, all desperate to play football and puzzled as to why they were not allowed to. Just as Owen had done, they asked their fathers to help them, and joined forces to set up a proper team. They were significantly better than Beaconsfield Youth Club, as Owen discovered when the two sides faced each other in the summer of 1970. She caught the eye of the Thame coaches, who asked her father if she would be interested in joining them instead and playing in the Oxfordshire League. She most certainly was, keen to develop her footballing skills and test herself against better opponents and with stronger team-mates. Of course, at the age of 16, Owen could not drive herself to Thame and back, so her chauffeurs every weekend were her father and one of the Beaconsfield Youth Club leaders, who split the 40-mile round trip.

After half a century, football authorities across the world had realised that their instructions to female players to put away their boots and stop their unladylike recreational activities were being ignored. Women had continued to play wherever they could, as much as they could. Without the support and structures of the men's football authorities, they set up their own organisations instead.

At around the same time that Wendy Owen and the girls in Beaconsfield and Thame were asking their fathers to help them set up football teams, in London a teenage Pat Gregory also wanted to play football. She took a different tack, and wrote a letter to the newspaper saying so. She did not expect a flood of responses from other girls and women, who also wanted to play and thought she was setting up her own team. Instead, she helped to set up an entire league and governing body – the Women's Football Association.

'My long-suffering parents!' she recalled. 'I'm in touch with another former officer of the WFA who lives in Spain, and he reminded me quite recently that we were in the same league together and we had the initial meetings of the league in my parents' front room.'

Her mother had no qualms about it, but her father was less supportive, not taking her to football with him until she was well into her teens, meaning she never got to go to a match at all before then.

'Obviously at 15 I wasn't allowed to go anywhere on my own,' she said. 'In those days I wasn't allowed to go to the cinema, for example.'

Gregory was completely unaware that women's football on affiliated pitches was banned, and had been for decades. When she took the first tentative steps to arrange matches and the doors were slammed in her face, it was her father – perhaps surprisingly – who was the most outraged.

'It was only at that point when the local council refused to deal with me that my father got cross,' said Gregory. 'He said, "They can't refuse to hire you a pitch or training facilities – I am a ratepayer!"'

The ban stood, though, so Gregory needed to find another way to go about pursuing her dream of playing football. She wrote another letter to the local newspaper about their lack of training facilities, and was contacted by a men's team from Tottenham called White Star, who offered to share their space. They told her that in the 1930s a men's amateur team called White Ribbon had trained alongside the Football League stars of Tottenham Hotspur, and that gave her the name for her new women's team – but they still were not able to hire a pitch or employ a referee, unless they were willing to run the risk of being removed from the governing body's list.

A now-notorious letter from the FA, signed by FA secretary Denis Follows and dated 21 July 1967, was intended to put these women off football, despite their enthusiasm and their newly founded club. 'As the Football Association does not recognise ladies' football teams, I am unable to inform you of any league to which you could apply for membership,' it read, somewhat primly. Gregory and her new White Ribbon team-mates were, of course, undeterred.

Gregory's next idea was to advertise in a football magazine, which had a two-fold impact. First, it was seen by boys' teams who were happy to play against White Ribbon if they could travel to their pitch – again risking the chance of disaffiliation from their county or their league for stepping on to a field with women and girls. Second, it was seen by a man named Arthur Hobbs.

In 1967, Hobbs was running an eight-team tournament for women's teams in Deal, and Gregory and White Ribbon travelled down to see them ('we were terrified, they were so strong, these teams,' said Gregory). It was the first inroad into establishing the Women's FA. The scattered teams developed the germ of an idea of setting up a governing body just for women's football, and Hobbs was instrumental, appointed as the WFA's first honorary secretary. Gregory referred to him as the organisation's 'founding father', mentioning in particular his great talent for dealing with the authorities and local politicians. The Deal tournament continued as the Women's FA found its feet; it was the officially recognised way for a team to become 'champions'. By 1969, there was interest from across Europe, with teams from Scotland, Czechoslovakia and Austria taking part. The evidence from participants' recollections and uncovered by researchers suggests that this was by no means the kind of tournament one might expect today; rather, it had truncated halves (10 minutes as opposed to the usual 45).

Gregory and her team were finally in an organised set-up, but as she admitted ruefully, it did not mean that they were on any path for future success.

'As with every sport I've touched, I'm never any good,' she noted with a laugh. 'I did score a goal once. It was from the halfway line and it was in Borehamwood, that's about all I can tell you, other than I kicked it – probably miskicked it. It went very high up in the air, the game stopped, we all looked at this ball, and it came down – because you had no nets, you had goalposts, but never nets.

'And the ball just went behind the goal, and that is such a unique goal, to me, I will remember it.'

In December 1969, while the Women's FA continued their independent organisation of matches, the FA Council began to think about a proposed resolution that women's teams should be allowed to affiliate to county associations if they wanted to. The FA were, however, at pains to point out that this did not mean they were encouraging women to play football. It was no surprise that the collective secretaries of county associations rejected the resolution in November 1970, voting it down by 21 votes to 13.

The county associations did not want to take on responsibility for women's football; nor did the international governing bodies, particularly, but they were concerned that teams were organising themselves, nation-, continent- and globe-wide competitions were taking place, and they had no control over them at all. UEFA and FIFA began to feel some worry about governing bodies for the women's game running their own international tournaments, beginning with the Women's World Cups from 1970 onwards, which were entirely unendorsed by the men's game's committees.

An edict was sent down to national federations telling them they needed to bring women's football into the fold to avoid the crisis of unregulated competitions. The FA Council agreed in November 1971 that they would meet with the Women's FA, thus acknowledging formally that women's football existed in England, and ultimately rescinding the ban. After that, the FA kept its distance from the Women's FA on an everyday basis, allowing them to continue running their leagues and competitions as they wished. Gregory, Hobbs and others involved in running the Women's FA were contacting governing bodies and the Sports Council to ask for funding or grants. What the FA's recognition did do, however, was allow links to be built up with UEFA and FIFA, and create an official England team.

'You have to remember that, of course, we were all honorary – we were doing this in our spare time,' she said, adding that Hobbs was a carpenter, and at the time she took on the role of the WFA's honorary assistant secretary, handling administration and correspondence, she was working full-time as secretary to the sports editor of the *Sunday Telegraph*. One of the next tasks on the agenda was to set up an official England team, which the FA and WFA discussed at a meeting in July 1972. After half a century of the game's repression, there were only around 4,000 players for any coach of an England women's team to choose from. FA coach Eric Worthington had been given the responsibility of selecting the inaugural squad. After the league sifted through the initial pool of players, the Loughborough College lecturer picked his squad of 25 at a final trial.

'The very first match, which was up in Scotland, we went by bus,' said Gregory, 'and we took 15 players – amongst whom was Wendy.'

When England came calling to ask her to go to trials for the first official women's squad, Wendy Owen did not think twice.

However, there was an obstacle in her way. As a student at Dartford, a women's PE college, she would need permission from the principal to be away from campus for a few days, and her classmates were not hopeful she would get it.

'They said, "Oh, you're going to have to get an audience. You're going to request an audience with the principal, and you need to ask her permission – and make sure you wear a skirt when you go!"

'I didn't have a skirt!'

Owen borrowed one from an older student, made the required appointment, and headed to the principal's house inside the college grounds.

'I sat down, I had my letter from the WFA, saying I've been selected for England. And she said, "Surely women playing football is just a joke?"

'I was going, "No, no, it isn't, we've had official trials, it's all properly organised, I've got the official letter here – women are playing football now, this is the first England team!"

'And in the end I was in her house for about 20 minutes, at the end of which she hadn't given me permission – she'd just said, "I'm going to have to take this matter to the governors."'

Owen was distraught. She had been through the gruelling and competitive trials and made it as far as the inaugural England squad, and now it looked like she might not be able to go at all. She spent a few days moping around campus, until one day she saw the principal in conversation with a stranger.

'She beckoned me over to the front of the college building, and just introduced me, all excited, and said to him, "This is Wendy Owen, this is the girl I told you about who's been selected for England!"' The stranger was the chair of the college governors and was much more impressed than the principal had seemed to be. 'At the end of that conversation I turned to her and said, "Does that mean I can go now then?"'

'She said, "Oh, yes." So obviously I was totally over the moon and that was that.'

Along with all the other invited players, she headed to Loughborough College – now Loughborough University – where manager Eric Worthington, who alongside his coaching work for the FA was one of the senior lecturers in PE there, could observe them and see who he thought was appropriate for selection.

'The FA actually appointed him,' recalled Owen. 'Although the WFA did everything else, they did get the FA to agree to appoint him and pay the expenses of the England team manager.

'After we were successful and after we got through, we were sent an international team circular, from Eric Worthington . . . saying he wants to remind us of the work we did during that training weekend and particularly the fitness – because we had to get ourselves fit, we only met up like the day before an international. We would have one day probably, a little bit of training with the team before an international, so [the coach] just did like set plays and stuff like that, not [fitness] training.

'I remember the manager after him [John Adams] just carrying on with that and [he] actually used to give us a fitness test when we arrived, and if we didn't pass the fitness test, we wouldn't be picked for the [starting] 11.'

Fifteen-year-old goalkeeper Sue Whyatt was also in those first England trials. She had started playing football with the boys in her street, and had joined Macclesfield Ladies, her local team, who trained on a cinder pitch.

'I took it in my stride,' she recalled. 'I never even told my mum and dad until the letter came through [inviting her to join the squad] – they didn't know what was going on.'

Whyatt had not expected anything from the trials. She had not been playing football that long, and Macclesfield Ladies were not one of the biggest or most successful teams, meaning as a goalkeeper she had conceded lots of goals, which she thought might put the England coach off selecting her.

'I was in awe of most of the other players because I was so young, I think,' she said. 'I was lucky – one of the other girls I played with at Macc was Janet Bagguley from Buxton – Janet Clarke now – so we went everywhere together.'

As well as asking them to monitor their pulse rate to see how quickly and how effectively they were recovering from strenuous activity, Worthington gave his players two sets of exercises to do: shuttle runs and mixed interval training that combined running, jogging and walking in turn.

'I used to go out and I'd do it by lamp-post,' said Owen. 'So I walked to the first lamp-post, jogged to the second one, and I'd run to the third one. I'd do it like that, running, jogging, walking along the street.

'I lived on a council estate where it was built around the green, where we used to play as kids. It was quite a reasonable-size green, so I used to set the shuttle running up on there.

'It was up to us to do that and come to the England matches fit. They didn't have time to do anything like that with us.'

Sheila Parker, whose grown-up status as a wife had very much impressed young Sue Whyatt, was England's first captain when they faced Scotland in Greenock. Parker was the married name of the little girl Sheila Porter, who remained a key part of the Fodens squad in the eight-team North West Women's league.

'It was good just leaving your hometown because in those days you didn't – it wasn't done,' she said.

Lining up for the national anthem was one of the most emotional experiences of the players' lives. They were the first women to play for an official England team; they had had no female role models to emulate when they were growing up. Hearing the strains of the famous tune played before kick-off made it all sink in, somehow.

'That was the best part,' said Parker.

Owen was only a substitute for England's first official match, which she remembered fondly regardless. 'That was a fantastic experience, that first match,' she said. A few days prior to that, the squad had visited Wembley Stadium for a media call, in an effort to engender some positive publicity for the England team's official debut. That was when Owen was snapped in the dressing room, applying the make-up that she would never usually put on prior to a game – or even away from football, not being keen on cosmetics in general. The eyeshadow palette and compact mirror were given to her to use as props by the reporter on the look-out for a great photo opportunity, and inevitably at that time it was going to be about the players' looks rather their skill.

'On the visit to Wembley, although we weren't allowed to play, we were allowed to stand on the football pitch and see the men's dressing rooms and stuff,' said Whyatt. 'I saved a bit of turf off the bottom of my boots from standing on the Wembley pitch for years and years and years until I found this little mouldy plastic bag with dust at the bottom.'

Owen made her full debut against France in 1973. The squad met up in Lea Green, Derbyshire, the day before they were due to fly out, and were met with an immediate challenge.

'As soon as we arrived we were told we were going to have this shuttle run fitness test – we had to do these reps of the shuttle runs, and if we didn't or we couldn't do them, we wouldn't be picked,' she said. 'Some of the girls hadn't been doing enough training and were going to throw up afterwards in the hedge. I made sure I'd done it. I'd been doing my reps and I was all right, so I got picked because I was determined – that wasn't going to stop me.'

Owen had been abroad twice before her England debut – once with her father's youth club trip to Majorca, and once to France with Thame Ladies. But travelling and staying abroad with England was entirely different.

'I think that's where my fear of flying first started,' she said wryly, recalling the tiny propeller plane on which they made the journey. 'We stayed in a girls' boarding school – two rows of beds facing each other – and the officials had to sleep together too in a dormitory.

'I remember being very nervous in the dressing room – and the toilet facility was a hole in the ground, which didn't help. We had about 3,000 spectators, so that was big for us. I don't know how many people we had in Scotland, but it wasn't anything like that. We tended to have much bigger crowds abroad than we did in England.'

The post-match refreshments were also out of the ordinary – a five-course banquet, although some of the food was somewhat shocking to the players, particularly the younger ones, who had no idea with what they had been presented.

'I do remember going over to France and the food being absolutely awful,' recalled Whyatt. 'We couldn't believe it. "What's this?!" They had these big silver tureens out, and it was like a lettuce leaf soaked in vinegar. Obviously now we know it's salad with French dressing, but then [it was], "Why are they giving us lettuce for our dinner?"'

The players themselves were paying for the privilege to travel and represent their country, as the Women's FA had little money of their own. It was what Owen described as a 'completely shoe-string budget'; clubs' affiliation fees and a small grant from the Sports Council were all they were operating on at first.

'We did get a bit of sponsorship that first match from Mitre Sports,' said Owen. 'I remember we had a free pair of football boots, which we thought was amazing, and a Mitre Sports bag for that first international, and they sponsored the equivalent of the Women's FA Cup now – in those days under the WFA it was originally the Mitre Cup.'

Over the intervening decades, Owen kept her correspondence from the Women's FA, offering an insight into the way the governing body communicated with their international representative team. For the second official match, requiring travel to France, the WFA confirmed they were seeking sponsorship but, failing that, they would be asking for contributions from players to cover accommodation and travel, although the younger girls like Owen who were at school or college would be exempt from compulsory financial outlay.

'I'd never been abroad,' recalled Whyatt, 'and we had to pay towards the travel costs, which was really hard for my mum and dad, and a lot of mums and dads, I'm sure – and I imagine those that were working, even, [like] Sheila Parker, with a family to look after. We were all working-class girls, needless to say.'

The players were allowed to celebrate post-match with a few drinks, which was normal – as long as they didn't go overboard. The younger girls – Whyatt included – sometimes bent the rules of the camp.

'I think Eric Worthington was very professional and set us on a good path, really,' she said. 'Then we had Mr [John] Adams after that. I have to say I preferred him – I think it was because Eric was more with the grown-ups. Mr Adams did realise that we were teenagers and needed a bit more discipline sometimes. I think Eric expected us to behave like grown-ups. But sometimes we didn't, I have to say!'

Whyatt revealed that sometimes the younger girls would sneak out of the team hotel at night to go dancing – and once at Bisham Abbey, a men's professional team were training there at the same time. 'They lowered a crate of beer out of their window down to us,' she recalled. 'We ended up going to a bit of a disco with them as well!'

It was unsurprising that it was a tough job keeping them all in line.

'Pat Gregory didn't know half of what was going on until well after the event,' admitted Whyatt.

'One of them quite recently said to me that they didn't real-ise I was the same age as them,' agreed Gregory. 'They thought I was much older.'

It was Gregory who had the responsibility for making players stick to the rules, and it was her name on the letters sent to them outlining the conduct and dress standards that would be required of them while on England duty. She and the rest of the Women's FA officials were very aware that they needed to pre-serve and strengthen their relationship with the FA, still in its very earliest stages and rather tentative. Trust was required on both sides, and it was Gregory's mission to ensure that the England players behaved in an appropriate fashion. That included smart and typically feminine clothes when off the pitch on international duty.

'I think we needed to be firm on the appearance we gave,' she explained. 'If we could have said to the Football Association, for example, "Stuff you, we're going to be the Women's Football Association of Great Britain and Northern Ireland" . . . but I think there was enough common sense around among the people who were trying to get this established that they realised there was no point alienating the authorities to that extent. I suppose telling the girls to wear skirts was what we thought they should do.'

Sheila Parker's first son was born in 1974, but nevertheless she continued to play football, continued to wear the England cap-tain's armband, and also continued her work as a receptionist.

Owen spent the next years partnering Parker in the centre of defence, but her international career came to an end at the age of 23 when she began to suffer repeated neck problems.

'I just had ongoing problems really,' she explained. 'When I first started playing, I didn't play centre-half, centre-back – I played for Thame and I was right-back for a lot of the time.

But then I became centre-back, and I was centre-back all the time for England. There's a lot of heading involved when you play centre-back. I was heading balls direct from the goal, opposite opponents' goal kicks, so I'd be on the halfway line, the goalkeeper would kick it half of the length of the pitch, I'd put my head on the end of that, and then corners would be coming in.

'I was picked for my heading ability because I was really good – that was my strength, my heading ability – so corners would come in and defensively I'd be heading them away, [and] I was sent up for attacking corners because I was good at heading.

'So I'd say most of my game, a lot of it was played in my head rather than my feet, and I got some neck problems, started to get these headaches. I do worry now [when you read] in the press about dementia – people, former footballers, heading all the heavy balls and things like that. In the end, I was getting headaches that were lasting from one week to the next.'

All the hospital could advise was a prescription of painkillers, but Owen was aware that continuing to play was likely to be creating problems in later life for her. Although the annual England trials were still open to her, she opted to concentrate on club football. By then she was playing for Maidstone and had moved back to sweeper, where she cut down on her heading entirely.

She continued playing at club level for a while, and also launched what became a very successful coaching career, combining it with school teaching.

'I wanted to start a girls' football team at school, and I was told I couldn't,' Owen said. 'I was actually discouraged from doing that, and told it wasn't considered to be a suitable game for the girls to be involved in, but if I wanted to coach the boys' team I could.

'I should probably have challenged that, but it was my first year [of teaching]. As a young teacher in your probationary year, you're not going to start arguing. I coached the under-13 boys for a couple of years.'

The turning point for Owen's coaching career came in 1978, when she was asked to go to the USA and coach at the Tampa Bay Rowdies soccer camp. This was a very big deal – Tampa were a huge name in the North American Soccer League, and were even featuring on British television.

'The local press came to my school to take photos,' recalled Owen. 'My boys were really impressed with that, and I think the school probably liked the publicity of it too.'

Owen chose to move into higher education shortly after that, lecturing at top PE college Leeds Carnegie, with her CV including the WFA preliminary coaching certificate she had been awarded in 1974. Her tutor on that course had been her one-time England manager Tommy Tranter, who acted as one of her references on her job application, and spoke highly of her coaching abilities. While at Carnegie she featured on an Open University programme, teaching a group of female students.

'Carnegie was by then mixed,' she said. 'It had been a men's PE college, but it had now got female students, and the lectures were all mixed. I was the only one of the females [on the teaching staff]; there were two women and the rest were men at Carnegie at that time. I certainly got some kudos being on that Open University programme.'

In 1981, she attended a preparatory course for what was then the top FA coaching badge, the Full Licence, which required a recommendation from a tutor before enrolment. Owen was unsure whether she would get the go-ahead as she was the only woman on the preparatory sessions.

'When I was on the FA prelim, I was the only female. The UEFA B licence, I was the only female again. And then when I went on the A licence there was me and one other female, one of my ex-England colleagues, but it was only two [women],' she said. 'You always felt like you'd got to be better than twice as good as anybody else to get it. The blokes on the course were very supportive, I have to say; there was never any problem like that. Some of the tutors, maybe you thought you'd got to win this lot over. So it is a pressure, because if you're the only one or there's only two of you on an all-male course it is difficult.'

Owen wrote a book in 2005, looking back on her footballing career and expressing her hopes for the future as well as making some predictions. One of her big dreams was for girls and young women to get the female role models she wished she'd had in her own youth.

'I think that has got a bit better now,' she mused. 'Female coaches at the World Cup 2019 – 9 out of 24 managers were female, one better than 2015, [where] 8 out of 24 managers were female, so 37.5% of coaches at the 2019 World Cup were women. The rest were men.

'Forty-one women A licence holders in England in 2017, 1,672 males. Obviously Hope Powell [was] the England manager from 1998 to 2013 but since then we've got male coaches [in charge of England, until the appointment of Sarina Wiegman in the autumn of 2021]. The more money comes into the sport, [the] more males are becoming interested in applying for the job, and if you're not careful, the female coaches get squeezed out of the game.'

Sue Whyatt, one of the youngest players in the first England squads, went into uniform not long after she left school. Aged 17, she became a police cadet; aged 19, she was a police officer. She had also been offered the chance to join the RAF, but opted for Cheshire Constabulary as she had been assured she would be able to continue playing football alongside her work.

It did not transpire that way. Although she would have been allowed time off to play for England, she was not allowed time off to play for her club side, Macclesfield Ladies, which meant she could not keep her skills primed.

'The lads all got time off for football, cricket, the band, everything, but I was the only female,' she said. 'They were like, "What if a rape comes in? Who's going to deal with that? You need a woman for that. What if we get women and children coming in? Lads can't deal with that." I hadn't got any children! The lads had got kids – why could they not deal with the kids? So basically they stopped me from playing.

'At the time, you just get on with it. Now, I feel very aggrieved. I wouldn't have put up with it now.'

She carried on playing football for the men's team at work, and tried other sports too, including netball, hockey and athletics. She was the first female dog handler in Cheshire, and then the first female dog sergeant in the country. Now a grandmother, she has been interested to see the sports the younger generation take up without thought of gendered expectations.

'Boys play netball, girls play football and it's all fine,' she mused.

FIVE

THE GOALSCORER

'MY EARLIEST MEMORY IS BEING in the back garden at my mum's, and she was always kicking a football around.'

Carol Parry, Sylvia Gore's cousin and close friend, shared plenty of memories with her. 'She used to come up quite a lot when I first got married and I had my daughter Laura. She loved Laura to bits,' said Parry. 'She was there quite a lot in the early days when Laura was growing up, trying to teach her to play football as well – but she was never into it!'

Gore could have taught little Laura plenty, with a magnificent footballing career. Her name was written in the history books after scoring England's first-ever official goal in the first-ever official match against Scotland back in 1972, sprinting half the length of the pitch in the pouring rain to sidefoot home.

That famous and historic goal is a snapshot of a stellar playing career. Indeed, the patchy records of the time suggest that Gore once netted 134 times in a single season. It was just one of her achievements during a storied footballing career, which began as a child watching her father and uncle play the game for Prescot Cables and wanting to follow in their footsteps. With no girls' teams in their hometown, as a 12-year-old she had a trial with the famous Manchester Corinthians.

Records now suggest that the Manchester Corinthians grew out of the hotbed of women's football in the North West that enjoyed a post-Second World War resurgence. Manager Percy

Ashley wanted to give his daughter Doris a team to play in, and he began to build a club to that end, attracting already-successful players from good teams in the area and further afield. He created a club and a series of teams that travelled and impressed the world.

'I played with Corinthians for a couple of years. We were the ones that went to Germany and won the European Cup.'

Veronica Bailey was talking about the start of her football career almost in passing. Macclesfield born and bred, she joined the Corinthians in 1957, and played there only for a couple of years before she had to leave school, get a job, and leave the game behind.

'My mum was a keen sportsperson, playing tennis and that, but of course we didn't have any football teams around here,' she recalled. 'Most of them that were about, like Manchester Corinthians, I think they formed about seven years before I went to play for them. You've heard of Dick, Kerr and that, but we never played against them – that was a bit before our time. But there was Fodens Ladies, Sandbach, teams all over the place that we gradually found out about. And when you're just in a little poky old town you really don't know nothing.'

Bailey's father had played football, and as a child she was allowed to go to the playing field at the bottom of the garden and kick a ball around with the local boys. When she was 14, she began her association with Corinthians, slotting into the first team immediately, and got to travel abroad for the very first time. They played a fundraising tournament in Portugal in two consecutive years, plus a week's tour of Spain. The little cup that Bailey treasured, however, was the one that was dubbed the European Cup, given to the winners of a four-team tournament in Germany. The memory was particularly special because the squad spoke to the legendary Germany and

50

Manchester City goalkeeper Bert Trautmann on the plane as he was en route to the same tournament, and he was happy to offer them advice.

'Money was scarce – you're talking about the '50s,' she said. 'Luckily my mum and dad got me some spends. Quite one hell of an experience, that.'

Bailey was massively proud that there was footage of the tournament widely available as well via Pathé News, even if it was not an entirely accurate portrayal of what happened. Germany were due to play Austria, who were unable to make the kick-off time, so Corinthians, who had already played and beaten a team from the Netherlands that day, were asked to step in and play a 20-minutes-each-way exhibition for the cameras.

'They didn't show any of the final or anything – it was a bit of a piss-take!' she laughed. 'They selected certain things that they just wanted to show on there, but you could tell it wasn't a proper match because we weren't in our own strip.

'I think it was a draw. I can't remember, to be honest. But the kid at the end, heading the ball, or trying to head the ball – that's me.'

When Sylvia Gore was too young to travel to training or matches alone, her parents John and Eileen would accompany her on lengthy bus journeys. When she was slightly older, she gave up her clerical job, packed her passport and travelled around the world with the Corinthians, playing exhibition matches, similar to the grand tradition and trail blazed by the Dick, Kerr Ladies.

She later joined the famous Fodens Ladies, set up at a lorry manufacturers in Sandbach, Cheshire, who became one of the most successful teams in England, culminating in winning the Women's FA Cup in 1973/74. The women there who founded the team were fortunate in the company's attitude towards their workers' recreation; they were keen to provide opportunities for sport and art and music, including establishing a very popular brass band. In May 1963, a new sports club opened, with a cricket pitch, a bowling green and tennis courts as well as indoor space for cue sports and badminton. There was, of course, also a football pitch, but this was not on the same campus. It is perhaps unsurprising to note that all these sporting provisions were intended for the male employees, with the women laying on tea, cake and refreshments.

The launch of the Fodens Ladies is somewhat obscured by the lack of attention given to them in the company documentation. Some researchers have suggested that they began playing in the middle of the 1950s, with their first match a challenge thrown down by Manchester Corinthians. One match programme from 1972 gives their founding date as 1957; the Fodens recreation club chairman said in 1975 that they were founded in 1959; while the club secretary in 1963 said they had formed only in 1961. An exact date is perhaps unimportant, though, when compared to their achievements.

Although initially a works team, certainly by the middle of the 1960s it was accepted practice for Fodens to name players who were not employees at the firm. Indeed, one of their rising stars was Jeannie Allott, a schoolgirl from Crewe, who shone in 1966 as a ten-year-old and eventually played in the first official England team six years later. Being able to recruit players who were not employees was beneficial to the general standard of the team and stopped them from losing squad members in tandem with staff turnover. Having said that, in the 1960s, Fodens were playing at carnivals and public events, often against men's teams or somewhat makeshift celebrity sides, indicating that it was not a massively serious endeavour at that point.

By the end of that decade, though, Fodens were successful and famous enough to become a de facto England side, in the way that Dick, Kerr Ladies had done before them. There is even a notorious photograph of an England v. Scotland challenge match featuring Fodens that seems to have been staged for publicity purposes: Joan Tench is rising for a header with Mary Davenport of Scotland's Westthorn United, and Jean Ramsey of Scotland is tugging Tench's shorts down to expose her underwear. Much like that staged photograph of Wendy Owen brushing on some make-up, it is the kind of vague titillation that ran underneath most of the press coverage of women's football at this time and beyond, where reporters and photographers were at pains to remind readers and viewers that these were women first and foremost, underneath their androgynous football kit.

The Butlins Cup, however, was the turning point for them. A tournament inspired – perhaps somewhat bizarrely – by the presenter of TV talent show *Opportunity Knocks*, Hughie Green, women's teams would travel to a Butlins camp to play a series of matches once every two weeks, resulting in an 'All-England Final'. Fodens first won the competition in 1969, beating Southampton 5–1 at Minehead in Somerset, and went on to face a Scottish representative side later in the year. As a result, they were often referred to as the 'British champions' despite the Butlins Cup not being recognised by the Women's FA – only non-affiliated teams took part.

Fodens were later affiliated to the WFA, and took part in their Mitre-sponsored Challenge trophy. In 1974, they thrashed Suffolk Bluebirds 9–2 in the quarter-finals, then beat Swindon Spitfires 2–0 in the semi-finals, but their opponents in the final, Southampton, were likely to prove a much sterner test – after all, they had won the trophy for the previous three years. In the showpiece event at the Bedford Eyrie in April 1974, Fodens beat Southampton 2–1, and boasted four internationals – including Sylvia Gore – in their line-up.

Despite their success, the company still did not give them the same kind of adulation that the men's sports teams might have got with the same achievements; indeed, although the Ladies had use of the bus, that was only if it was not required by the brass band. Of course, the players had to pay for their own accommodation and food when they were travelling to matches. Their international tours were covered in the company newsletter, but instead of focusing solely on their sporting achievements, there was invariably a focus on what fine ambassadors they were for the firm.

After suffering a disabling back injury which forced her into retirement, Gore worked tirelessly as an adult volunteer to create a structure for girls to play football at local level, setting up and coaching teams in the North West of England, with future Lionesses Rachel Brown-Finnis and Sue Smith among those who benefited from her knowledge. She was part of the Women's FA, who organised and ran women's football in England before the FA took over in 1993, after which she sat on their women's committee and then served as a delegate for the Women's Super League, launched in 2011. She was also the first female director of the Liverpool County FA.

Wendy Owen coached with Gore at the turn of the millennium, having encountered her plenty of times before they became England team-mates – most notably at the Butlins Cup All-England final in September 1970, where Owen's Thame faced Gore's Fodens.

'Obviously I knew Sylvia as an opponent, and then she was a member of the first England squad, so I got to know her [personally],' said Owen. 'She was about 27, 28 at the time, [and] I was only 18 . . . we weren't really close pals then because we were ten years apart.

'But then, later on, she got me involved at Tranmere Rovers Centre of Excellence for girls, 1999 to 2001. She was the coordinator of the centre, and she knew I was local, so she asked me to come and coach the under-16s at Tranmere Rovers. She was helpful in getting me involved in some of those first things I did when the game was getting off the ground a bit more.

'She could get her voice heard . . . She was dynamic. I think she did relate well to the players, I think that they liked her. She could get things done, get things going. And she was very involved – and a lot of it was voluntary.'

'You never saw her in a skirt unless she was going somewhere posh – she was always in a tracksuit, Sylvia, she had a wardrobe full of tracksuits, I think,' smiled Parry. As she was 13 years younger than her cousin and so did not see her play in her prime very much, she had often watched her coaching.

'I remember going to Prescot Grammar and there was a big tournament on,' she recalled. 'She'd gone to see if there was any talent there, and it was a nice sunny afternoon. There were lots of games going on, she was walking round, and again when I went with her there, the amount of people who went up to her and chatted with her, and recognised her – when I think back I didn't realise at the time she was well known within that area of coaching and spotting talent.'

Gore did not talk too much about her achievements in football. Only in passing did her family learn about what she had done.

'I've never known anyone who liked her food so much,' laughed Parry, 'but she did, she loved her food, and so she'd always arrive at mine at crucial times like lunch or evening meals, and we'd sit down and chat and talk about normal things, about dogs and gardens, and she might mention just a fleeting moment about what she'd done that week with football.'

Parry added: 'There was a video on YouTube of her being the first woman to score for England – and she said, "Look at me! Look how much weight I've put on! Look how slim I was there."'

Gore's endeavour was recognised by the footballing authorities and the government. In 2000, she was awarded a special achievement prize by UEFA, and collected an MBE from Prince Charles at Buckingham Palace. The year prior, she had been honoured at the first-ever FA Women's Football Awards; she later returned to the Palace in 2013 to meet Prince William and collect another award for her contribution to women's football as part of the FA's 150th anniversary celebrations. She was inducted into the National Football Museum's Hall of Fame in 2014 alongside stars of the men's game including Alan Shearer, Patrick Vieira and Trevor Francis.

Gore revelled in the spotlight, as one might expect from such an eye-catching player and successful coach. Her cousin Carol went to Monaco with her as her guest to collect her prize from UEFA, and they had a wonderful trip, with Gore in her element spotting famous faces and talking football with as many people as possible.

'On the plane going over, Alex Ferguson [then the Manchester United manager] was on there,' Parry reminisced. 'He was in first class, and when we got off we were supposed to catch the helicopter, as there was a helipad at the hotel, but there was only one [helicopter] in service that day, and he took it over and she was livid. We then had to get a bus into Monaco! It was a bit of a disappointment. Fancy him being on the same plane and we had to go and get the bus because he's in the helicopter! That was really funny.

'The ceremony was really good, it was lovely; she wasn't fazed by it at all, she was so not nervous at all. I'm not saying she was over-confident but she wasn't nervous at all. She seemed to enjoy the recognition, I think.'

The two spent a beautiful few days in Monaco, and even got some sight-seeing in. Parry did not necessarily find sharing a room with her cousin particularly relaxing, though. 'She snored like a trooper, and I actually slept in the bath for two nights with a couple of cushions!' she said. 'I couldn't wake her up, she was a good sleeper, so I slept in the bath of this lovely hotel room.'

Parry was also Gore's guest when she went to collect her MBE as well, along with her aunt and uncle. 'By mistake the guy on the [hotel] desk gave my aunt and uncle the suite, which we were supposed to be in – it was a proper lounge, sitting room, bedrooms, bathrooms. We were downstairs where the servants were!

'We stayed where we were, and let my aunt and uncle enjoy it. That was just a funny thing, we laughed about it instead.'

Parry and her aunt and uncle had to leave Gore when they arrived at Buckingham Palace; the recipients were in a different room to the guests. Gore was not best pleased with the hospitality on show, though.

'There was no drinks or anything to eat!' said Parry. 'We must have been there about five or six hours waiting for everyone else to go through, and she said, "I can't believe we've been in the Palace and nobody's offered us a glass of water."

'It was a really long day, and there was nothing there at all. She just didn't understand why nobody had come round with sandwiches and a drink. It's a long time!

'When we were coming out of the Palace, we got a taxi, and going through the gate there were all these people, tourists. She said, "Sit up straight and wave like the Queen – they might think we're royalty!"'

Gore accepted the role of Manchester City ambassador on International Women's Day in 2016. Though the professional incarnation of Manchester City did not exist as a women's team when Gore was playing, they certainly shared a tradition with Corinthians, who she served so adroitly for so many years.

'I'm delighted to be their ambassador – not because they're successful but because the whole club is run in a professional way: men's, women's, juniors,' she said in 2016. 'Everything is spot-on. I can't fault it at all. I'm really honoured to be part of that.'

Gore had begun walking with a crutch due to increasing back pain, which had been diagnosed as sciatica. After the injury that had limited her mobility earlier in life, she was used to discomfort, but this really cut down her activity. She still tried to kick a ball, though.

'I remember her going to walking football – she had a little go at that,' recalled Parry. 'That was hilarious because she wanted to run! That was not a good idea.'

She had started to put together plans to be reunited with her old Manchester Corinthians team-mates, to be held at the end of the 2016 Women's Super League season, in full expectation that City would be parading the championship trophy by then. Gore did not live to see the Blues' maiden WSL title win. After a short illness, she died in September 2016, aged 71.

'Do you know what really shocked me when she died? I didn't realise how many lives she'd touched,' said Parry. 'She was very humble, Sylvia, really, and although the major things she won she celebrated, because that was a massive achievement for her, underlying that there were all these girls she coached and inspired. I didn't realise to what depth that was. When she passed, I was shocked by the amount of people who got in touch to say what a massive impact she'd had on their career and their life.

'I found that quite sad, because I was thinking, "Did I not talk enough about football?" Although I taught PE, football wasn't my game – it was hockey, my game . . . I was thinking, "Oh my God, I didn't realise how many people knew her."'

Gore left Parry's daughter Laura her MBE in her will.

Over a decade after Veronica Bailey stopped playing for Corinthians, she had put on her boots again, and helped to set up Macclesfield Ladies at the inception of the Women's FA.

She was working in a factory in the town, and one of her female colleagues was keen on football. Finding out that Bailey had played previously, she set up a local kickabout, and plenty of girls and young women turned up.

'We were very lucky because the amount of people that turned up were people that were really very good!' she recalled. 'And when we decided that we would form a football club properly, we had a secretary, treasurer, a chairman and everything, as you would have on a proper committee. So there were a lot of people involved with it – we had a school teacher who could arrange training facilities in the gym and things like that.'

The newly formed Macc Ladies played against some very strong opposition, including Sylvia Gore and her Fodens team. Bailey even joined Gore's squad when they toured Belgium in 1977, scoring twice in their opening fixture, against Cercle Brugge KSV, which ended in a 4–4 draw.

'Sylvia!' Bailey recalled. 'She was a damn good player. She played on the wing . . . They were obviously a lot more experienced than Macclesfield because [of] most of the girls when we started, I think there was only me that [had] actually played before, for a proper team.'

She admitted that she had missed football in some ways – but not in others. 'You start getting boyfriends and your life takes different meanings at times and I had missed football,' she said. 'We'd always watched football. The beauty of forming the club as well, you get new friends too, and from a lot of that develop friendships.'

The creation of Macc Ladies was very special to Bailey, even compared to her earlier achievements with Corinthians. For the next 15 years, Bailey and Macclesfield Ladies competed in their local leagues and trophies as well as playing fundraising matches. They even played on the men's famous Moss Rose ground to raise money for the club.

'We had some amazing people and they should all be really very proud of themselves – it wasn't just me,' she said. 'I wouldn't have done that on my own, it was just some wonderful people.'

When Bailey decided to retire from playing, though, the club folded, much to her surprise. She was the oldest player by around ten years and wanted to stay fit enough to pursue other interests, including long-distance running. 'When I said I was packing in, everybody else packed in,' she said. 'It was just a bit disappointing, really.'

Her retirement from playing was a busy one. As well as running the People's Marathon in Birmingham in 1981, she also took up mountain climbing, reaching the summit of Ben Nevis twice, and Scafell Pike and Snowdon numerous times. In 2019, she was pleased to be reunited with some of her old Corinthians team-mates at the National Football Museum in Manchester.

'We sang the old Corinthians song!' she recalled happily. Bailey claimed she was not much of a singer, but she remembered all the words.

We're Corinthians from Manchester, football ladies of Lancashire
Blue and white for Corinthians, oh, what a team
We'll beat anyone who we play,
Makes no difference at home or away
We have the talent, our youngsters are gallant
Corinthians of Manchester!

After a busy life and plenty of hobbies, travel and friendship, at the age of 78, Bailey had no more ambitions. 'I think as you get older, your body gets a bit more tired,' she said. 'I always tell my friends, if I pop my clogs now, I've no complaints.'

SIX

THE FORGOTTEN

BEFORE THE OFFICIAL ENGLAND TEAM played their first games, a more controversial representative team had travelled the world in the years previously.

The players in that squad had no idea how much scandal they would cause simply by playing football. Like Pat Gregory, Sylvia Gore, Wendy Owen, Sue Whyatt, Sheila Parker and the others, they had started kicking a ball around while the sport was still supposedly banned for women in England.

Chris Lockwood was born in Yorkshire, moving down south at a young age, and though she had two sisters, all she ever wanted to do was play football with her male cousins.

'I didn't like any other sport but football,' she said. 'I used to play football with the boys all the time, because I didn't know any other girl that played football. At senior school I couldn't wait to get out of school, really, to meet the boys and play football, and this girl said to me, "We're starting up a girls' football team, a women's football team." And I went, "What, really?" I didn't know there was any other women that played. And she said, "Yeah, come along," so I went along.'

None of Lockwood's team-mates was particularly talented, but they were keen, and it was a good way for her to show off her skill. Soon one of the Women's FA founder members came calling; Harry Batt, manager of Chiltern Valley, invited her to join his team. Lockwood was only 13 then, but there were other youngsters in the Chiltern Valley squad – Leah Caleb for one.

Caleb grew up in Luton, and her football skills had been noticed by her headmaster, who wanted her to join the boys' team. She was not allowed, and instead at the age of 11 joined Chiltern Valley, based at the Crawley Green Recreation Ground. She took two buses across town every week to get to training, where she was unsurprisingly one of the youngest.

As one of the WFA's founder members, Harry Batt was well known to other people in women's football around the world. He was invited to bring along his side to an international tournament in Italy in 1970, featuring eight teams from across the world, and then in 1971 he was asked if he could bring a team to an unofficial World Cup in Mexico. The country was ready to put on another major tournament, having hosted the men's World Cup the year before, so the organisers knew there were plenty of fans who wanted to watch top-quality football. Importantly, there were also plenty of big and financially successful brands on board to promote the competition and provide sponsorship money.

Batt took a squad to a qualifying competition in Sicily in June 1971, travelling by train across the continent, where they lost 7–0 to Italy in Trapani and then beat Austria 3–0 in Syracusa two days afterwards. That was enough to secure them a place in Mexico in August.

Caleb had been on the trip to Sicily and was all set for Mexico at the age of 13 and a half. 'I always stick the half in because 13 does sound so young!' she said.

Teenager Gill Sayell was on Batt's list for Mexico too. She had four brothers and two sisters, and began playing football in a field near their home in Aylesbury as a small child. It was not long before she was snapped up by a team – a boys' team. She kept her hair cropped short and went under the name 'Billy' until they realised she was a girl. Forced to leave, she learnt of Thame, the women's side based around 20 miles away from her home, and aged 12 she began playing for the reserve side, known as the Wanderers.

'That was 1970,' she said. 'The next year, we were playing an exhibition game in Aylesbury against Fodens, and we beat them, 5–3, I believe. And Harry Batt was there watching the game, scouting, and I was one to be picked. A couple of other girls were picked to go but they couldn't because of work commitments. As I was still at school, you know, that wasn't a problem – the problem was just having to rush around to get a passport because I'd never been abroad before!'

It was a gamble for everyone involved. The tournament's lack of approval from the official governing bodies meant it could quite easily rile them, even though they were not organising any international competitions for women themselves. In England, officially women were still not supposed to be playing on affiliated men's pitches at all. That was part of the reason why Harry Batt himself took care to call his team 'British Independents' rather than lay any claim to the England name and irritate the FA. Unsurprisingly, perhaps, the tournament organisers still called them 'Inglaterra', perhaps taking some kudos from having a team from the home of football, and it certainly did rile the authorities back at home.

'Harry had a struggle to get a team to go there, because he was struggling with the politics,' said Lockwood. 'He did a great job but of course we didn't have the support that the other teams that went in the finals had. He knew good players, and a lot of players that he wanted to take. I do know that [Scottish star] Rose Reilly, who was exceptional, was actually asked to go, but she was warned off by the Scottish FA at the time – but having said that, if some of the girls had gone I don't suppose me and Leah and Gill would have gone because we were quite young. So it was right place, right time for us.'

Indeed, Batt picked his squad mostly from his Chiltern Valley players – although many of his senior players were unable to take four weeks off work to travel overseas for football. The schoolgirls, meanwhile, were thrilled to have the opportunity to go abroad during their holidays, and got permission from their parents to go.

'They knew I was mad on it and they knew I was good,' said Lockwood. 'Harry and his wife June came to our house [to explain the trip]. And [my parents] knew that Leah was sensible – Leah was always sensible even though she was younger than me, and her mum and dad said yes, and my mum and dad said yes!

'Maybe we didn't know how far away Mexico was. We played in the qualifiers in Sicily earlier in the year – they'd let us go there and we got back in one piece – so they were very confident that June and Harry were looking after us, and we were looked after, really we were. Some of the girls in the team were RAF girls so they were used to looking after themselves, so there was never any dangerous moments.'

They might have been in the Royal Air Force, but they had never flown on a jumbo jet before; it was a new experience for everyone in the squad, who were fascinated to get a tour of the plane, including going upstairs and seeing the bar.

'I hadn't even been to an airport or anything,' said Sayell. 'I didn't really know any of the girls. Quite a few of them had played together anyway. I think I'd had about two training sessions with them before we went.'

'It was surreal,' said Lockwood. 'We had to go to New York first and we had to wait for the next plane to go to Mexico – and then when we got to Mexico it was really late at night. Only then, at that moment, did we know that we were quite famous there. Nobody said it was going to happen, we didn't know, and there was all TV cameras, police, that was it!'

'It must have been adrenaline just keeping us going,' added Sayell, thinking back to that long journey. 'When we were in JFK [airport], because we all had our walking-out suits on, nice little jackets and skirts and things, one lady asked if we were a choir – that was quite funny!'

People in Mexico knew who they were, though. The English players found themselves thrust into a world of celebrity. Their training sessions alone would attract hundreds of spectators.

'I think we were all taken aback by that,' said Sayell, 'because we didn't know what to expect. Coming from playing the football that we played here, with hardly anybody watching, to be in the limelight. It was great. Even in the mornings – we used to train about half seven in the morning, before it got too hot – we had crowds watching us then, about 200 people. They were allowed to sit along around the fence and everything to watch us play, so we were sort of pretty accessible to anybody, which I think that's what they all liked out there as well – they could get up close to the players. You couldn't really imagine it now.

'It was hot. I got a little diary, and I remember saying that the pitch is pretty hard and I had to have my rubber studs in and things like that. It was just sort of surreal that we were there.'

'We had a reporter with us the whole time taking photos,' said Caleb. 'Hence we have got memorabilia and our newspaper cuttings, so it helps you to remember. We went to the British embassy, to the ambassador's house, cocktail party. There was all sorts – television appearances. I went on television on my own!

'From what I can remember, it was just asking me things like did I like Mexico? And I was answering yes or no in Spanish.'

The matches themselves were very tough, as might have been expected with so many young teenagers in the side playing against fully grown women in the opposition. One of the teenagers, Yvonne Farr, broke a leg against Mexico; Carol Wilson fractured her foot.

'We had to play the Latin American teams – and it wasn't quite so, perhaps, helpful because they do play a different game,' said a diplomatic Lockwood.

'I didn't play in all of the matches,' said Caleb. 'I played in the Argentina game, and I think I did play a part of the Mexico game – it's quite difficult to [remember] because it was all played within 24 hours of each other.

'The other thing people are not understanding about those days and the football – we weren't tactically astute. We were a team that Harry pulled together . . . you look back at it and you think, "Good grief, we went in there without a big strategic plan." Really, we didn't know what we were going to be hit with.'

Nevertheless, the England team got to play in the Azteca Stadium, the pinnacle of many players' careers.

'It's mental, really, to think that we did that – absolutely crazy,' said Sayell. 'What I remember of that is coming from the changing rooms – they are underneath, so you come up a step out on to the pitch, so I found that quite fascinating . . . and then you just saw this massive big stadium in front of you, and the crowds are just crazy.

'I wish I'd been a bit older to appreciate what was going on more, because being 14, you can't – you take it in your stride, you don't really take in what's happening.'

At the last moment, the tournament organisers staged a fifth-place play-off between England and France to capitalise on the interest. By that time, six days after they had been knocked out of the tournament, Batt's team only had eight fit players, and they needed to borrow some personnel from Mexico. Janice Barton scored twice, but France won 3–2.

'In the grand scheme of things of playing in a stadium of that size, against Latin American teams, within 24 hours of each other, you start thinking, now you look back, "Actually, you know what, we didn't do that bad,"' said Caleb. 'We were gutted. I do think people don't realise – of course we wanted to win, we were very proud of being able to play for our country. Whether people were happy about it in England or not, actually it doesn't really matter, but we were on a stage [where] there was a lot of people interested in a team that came from England playing in a World Cup. You can't change that. It's quite amazing how the Mexican people just embraced us. We had a fabulous relationship with them – and that's before we played Mexico. We built up a very good relationship, and that stays with you forever. How lucky was I really to have that?'

On 5 September, Denmark won the World Cup, thanks to a hat-trick from 15-year-old Susanne Augustesen. The Danish Football Association refused to recognise the achievement as it was an unofficial tournament. The same thing happened to Batt's squad too when they returned to England – all of them were banned. The manager was banned for life, the older players were banned for six months, and the younger girls for a shorter period. Half a century on, the players did not remember it clearly.

'I can't remember a letter – I haven't got that, [and] I kept most of my bits and pieces,' said Sayell. 'My dad must have just said, "Well, you can't play for . . . I don't know how long it was." A couple of months, maybe.'

They did, however, remember the feelings of shame and humiliation they had.

'We've done what we've done out there,' Sayell said, 'and for them to ban us knocked [us] a bit because we thought we'd done something wrong. Instead of encouraging us, and to build on that competition and say, "Look, this is what can be achieved," we got knocked for it. And, you know, I think that that was probably, looking back now, the hardest thing. We should have been encouraged, really, and they could have built on that success of that competition.'

'We knew we were banned,' said Caleb, 'but I suppose it was coming into winter by the time they told us so probably we would have hardly played anyway because in those days you were on a park pitch.

'Chiltern Valley were the hotspot. Harry was such a forthright character, obviously a maverick, a man before his time.

Chris and I were both told it would be best if we didn't carry on playing for Chiltern Valley.'

While they were banned, the schoolgirls went back to kicking a ball around with their classmates. They were informed that if they wanted to continue playing, they would need to sign for another team affiliated with the Women's FA. Lockwood and Caleb both joined a team initially formed from a Luton telecoms factory, Daytel.

Sayell went back to Thame, stepping up to the first team, and played there until 1976, when her father set up Aylesbury Harlequins, later Aylesbury United.

'All I wanted to do was play football,' she said. 'I didn't get into the politics of things or anything like that – Dad dealt with anything that came along.'

Ultimately Chiltern Valley disbanded – not before another unauthorised trip to Italy. Looking back, Caleb wished she had been older, so she could have understood more of what was happening and been able to stand up for Batt.

'That was so unfair what happened,' she said. 'Even though, yes, he was a force of nature, he had a strong character, they should have embraced his character and taken it forward, not tried to take it away or bottle it for themselves. It's just ridiculous.'

Lockwood, Caleb and Sayell stayed firm friends but never spoke about their trip to Mexico.

'I did my scrapbook when I came back from Mexico, and I've looked at it once or twice and then put it away,' said Caleb. 'You really didn't talk about it. So it sat dormant for all those years.'

It was not until 2019 that they shared any of their memories. A BBC journalist had written a feature about the team they dubbed the Lost Lionesses, and the quest began to reunite that squad.

'It's quite bizarre,' said Lockwood. 'We just played for the now. When we had all that attention . . . a lot of us hadn't seen each other for 48 years. Well, we didn't feel strange to each other, there was that team spirit. We were slightly worried that there would be a sad story – to get 14 people, the ages we are now, it was wonderful, you know, we were all still alive! It was fantastic. That was our main aim, really, to reach out and find each other, and to give Harry the respect he deserved.'

Harry Batt was not at the reunion; he had died in 1985, without ever having been allowed back into women's football. His team, however, were feted by UEFA in France, with hospitality laid on for them as they watched the new generation of England players compete at the highest level.

'I can honestly say, I swear to it, I felt like we were the same people,' said Lockwood. 'I don't know how that is because obviously we've all had different lives, marriages or whatever, and yet, just, you know, we laughed at the same things. It was brilliant.'

Lockwood was shocked to find out that some of her teammates from 1971 had not resumed playing after their ban expired. 'Some of the girls packed up,' she said incredulously, 'so some girls, their very last football match was in the Azteca Stadium.'

Half a century after they crossed the world to play football, the so-called Lost Lionesses have finally achieved the recognition they deserve.

'A couple of times I've been in the shop or something and someone's come up to me – "Oh, you're the Lost Lioness girl!" laughed Lockwood. 'It's amazing. They've gone, "You really inspired my granddaughter, she loves football." Yes, that has been something I didn't expect and so I'm really glad just for that, if it inspires one or two to keep going.'

Lockwood herself admitted to a regret – that she stopped playing too early. 'I was in my late twenties, and I started doing shift work and I was in IT, and I was doing 12-hour shifts. And I wasn't turning up for training and I thought, "I can't have this, I've got a house, got a mortgage, and I gave it up. Whenever I speak to anybody now, I say play as long as you can because when you can't, you can always watch.'

Caleb stopped playing in 1991, just as the Women's FA introduced the ten-team National Premier Division. She was insistent that the achievements of that unofficial squad shaped women's football in the rest of the century, particularly as the ban on women's football was effectively lifted the year after.

'There is no coincidence about the changes of 1972,' she said. 'There is no doubt that Mexico in my head had an influence on that because of the magnitude of that tournament.'

SEVEN

THE ADVENTURER

'MY SISTER KEEPS ON TELLING me, you know. She says you were born 20 years too early.'

Pat Chapman was in reflective mood. Into her sixties and following a career spent with a national pharmacy chain, she was looking back on her days in football, when she starred for Southampton and later Red Star Southampton, and when she was presented with a stunning opportunity.

'When [England] played at Wimbledon against Italy [in November 1977] there was a centre-forward who played alongside me called Eileen Foreman,' she began. 'Now, afterwards, we were asked to go and speak to these two Italian blokes, so we thought we'd go, just to see what they had to say, so we went down there. Through an interpreter, we were asked to go to Italy to play professionally, and we declined.'

Chapman was in her very early twenties when this happened, and was fond of her home comforts, unlikely to want to venture into an entirely alien country.

'We were offered something like a flat and a car and about £100 a week. So you work that one out, how much that was worth. That would have been a lot. And I was asked to go to Germany to play professionally, and I turned that down as well, so I was born 20 years too soon.'

Chapman played alongside one of the first women to leave England and play domestic football overseas. Sue Lopez spent all but one season of her 20-year playing career with Southampton. That interregnum was spent in Italy, in 1971, where she played for Roma, albeit not as a professional – just receiving her expenses, sharing a flat with one of her team-mates, and enjoying a year playing on better pitches in front of bigger crowds. Lopez helped Roma to the League Cup during her spell there, enjoying the chance to play in front of thousands, and also getting to travel the world on tour with them.

Lopez was one of the faces of women's football at the time. In 1969, she had been part of the unofficial England side that went to the FIEFF's European Championships (unauthorised by UEFA). They finished third, and she was the tournament's top scorer. So many female footballers had been inspired by watching the England men win the World Cup in 1966; Lopez worked with some of that team's stars in campaigning for an equivalent women's tournament. She posed for promotional photos with hat-trick hero Geoff Hurst, in which they were jumping to challenge for a header – and Lopez rose the highest. Hurst, along with his club and country team-mates Bobby Moore and Martin Peters, were three of the leading lights in the push for a women's World Cup to be hosted in England, but it didn't happen. It was a major regret for Lopez, who could not help but wonder how women's football in England might have developed had the authorities, the media and more sponsors got behind the game in the 1970s.

She wrote in her account of the women's game that she found it a very easy decision to leave her secretarial job and go to Italy, where the sports newspapers carried match reports of the weekend's action, where teams worked on technique, and where referees handed out bookings for bad challenges rather than assuming that a woman could not have intended to commit a foul. However, her success with Roma meant that other top players – just as frustrated with the lack of formal backing for women's football in England – also considered relocating, and murmurs began to circulate that Italian clubs were deliberately 'poaching' players and offering them salaries and financial enticements.

This was ultimately what forced Lopez to, reluctantly, return to England from Italy. The rumour mill had been turning, with whispers and even some newspaper reports suggesting that she was being paid to play, even though she was only receiving expenses. However, there was a strong concern that playing abroad might compromise her amateur status – and if she returned to England at any point, that could in turn lose the WFA its crucial funding from the Sports Council, and further limit its ability to function effectively.

'We were told very clearly by the Football Association and by the Sports Council that the onus was on the player if and when they came back to this country to prove that they had not lost their amateur status,' said Pat Gregory. 'Any grant aid that [the Sports Council] gave was for the running of amateur sports. But of course it was a very different world then. We were told quite clearly [that] if we had in our membership any player who had become professional then we would lose the grant aid. It was that simple. And there was no way we were going to be that powerful that we could do anything other than that [tell Lopez to return to England and avoid any possibility of suggestions of professionalism] in order to carry on.'

Lopez admitted later that she had intended to go back to Italy in 1972, but the lure of being part of the first official England team proved too much. So instead of joining up again with Roma, she returned to Southampton and helped to shape the team into one of the most impressive forces in women's football. They had initially formed shortly after the 1966 World Cup. The Cunard Shipping Line workers had set up a team, and wanted opponents. Keen female footballers from the area met up on a local common and put together some casual sides, eventually creating Southampton Women. Unlike the men's team of the same name, the facilities were limited: no proper changing rooms or showers, a reliance on volunteers to run the club and officiate fixtures, and of course all costs were covered by the players themselves.

That was no bother. Lopez and her Southampton team dominated the FA Cup for a decade after its creation in 1970/71, appearing in ten of the first eleven finals and winning eight of them. In addition to that, Lopez won 22 caps during her career, in a time when international matches were infrequent. They were difficult to arrange, there were few opponents, and players were having to take time off work, before finding themselves out of pocket.

Some of those players are almost absent from the record books now, even though their achievements should be set down in permanent ink.

'I found the book with all the goals I ever scored!' enthused Chapman, who had been on a search of her loft. A prolific striker who served Southampton with distinction, she maintained that she should have been in the *Guinness Book of World Records* for her goalscoring feat in 1978, when she scored six goals in the WFA Cup final as Southampton beat QPR 8–2 at Slough Town.

'I sent them all the information,' she said. 'I sent them programmes, pictures from women's archives. I sent them everything. They had so much information, pictures, newspaper clippings. The reason why they wouldn't accept it – I couldn't get a letter confirming it from the Women's Football Association. Bit disappointing. But if you can carry an egg on your head for three miles you can get in.'

Chapman was prone to pre-match butterflies, particularly before important games, and she was nervous before that one.

'QPR were a great side – it was always very close. If you said before the game, "Who's going to win?" you'd have said, "Oh, it could go either way." But we scored early, Pat Davies scored early, and I remember, because I took the corner and she headed it in. And we scored early. And then we scored again.

'Then I got the third goal, and we were 3–0 up quite quickly, and I don't know what it was, I just relaxed a bit. And I remember – everything that touched my foot went in. It was just one of those days. It never happened again.'

She was an enthusiastic keeper of statistics and memorabilia, and had unearthed in her loft a treasure trove of history that she had almost forgotten even existed. 'I found all the programmes from the cup finals – loads of good stuff, actually, I was quite surprised. My old England cap I found, so that was quite good.'

Those England caps from the 1970s and 1980s were not the slick ones distributed to every player following professionalisation. They were handmade and stitched by Women's FA administrator Flo Bilton, with each player getting a single one. Chapman got a handful of other complimentary items during her playing days: one free pair of boots, a sweatshirt, and a tracksuit for training, which created its own problems. Due to her short stature, she had to roll up the trouser legs and jacket sleeves.

Chapman got her first call-up in 1976, and she discovered her selection for the squad to face Scotland at the Woodside Stadium in Watford courtesy of an unusual source. 'It was Sylvia Gore who rang me! She rang me at work at lunchtime, and she just said, "Hi, Pat, it's Sylvia," and I said, "Hi Sylvia, what are you ringing me for?" And she said, "I'm going to tell you something – you'll get your letter tomorrow."'

One of Chapman's favourite memories of her international career was playing Belgium at the Dell, then Southampton FC's home ground, which attracted high-profile local sponsors because of the number of local women in the England team. The Southampton men's manager Lawrie McMenemy was hugely supportive of the women's game, due in part to his friendship with Lopez, who was progressing through her coaching qualifications, and he lobbied for the England squad to be able to use their training ground in preparation. Thanks to him, the women also got to meet some famous faces.

'We were introduced to Ron Greenwood, who was then the [England] men's manager,' said Chapman. 'That's when you really, really felt proud. Yeah. I really felt proud.'

Chapman began her stellar career playing in a youth club team before being invited to join a friend's team, and then being scouted by Southampton in 1972 – ironic for someone who was a committed fan of their fierce rivals Portsmouth.

'There was none of this business of transferring all the people in from all over the place,' Chapman recalled. 'We were local girls. I travelled the furthest because I lived in Portsmouth [but] the Portsmouth team wasn't good enough. We spent a lot of money travelling. We always paid subs because the places where we had to train, we had to pay for. For a women's team we were very well supported because we were obviously at that time the best team in the country. But, yeah, we travelled all over the place on a minibus, played on Southampton Common where the pitches were dreadful. The balls were hard, the boots weren't like they are today, but it was just wonderful.'

Chapman attributed Southampton's success and dominance of an era to the players' simultaneous development. 'There was a group of us . . . that were all around the same age. That's why we were so good for so long, because we were all 16, 18 [when the squad was first put together]. [Sue] Lopez and [Sue] Buckett were the oldest but they were super fit and played well into their thirties.'

But the fact that the squad were all roughly the same age also contributed towards their downfall. Ultimately, they were victims of their own success.

'This is one thing we failed on a little bit, to be honest,' she admitted. 'Because there was a lot of us who were at that same age, we played all for about the same amount of time. You're talking about a team that had about eight or nine current international players . . . and most of the rest of us had played either regional level or at international level.

'It was a really difficult team to get into, so the youngsters didn't really want to come to us because they knew they weren't going to get a game, you see, and that's what was difficult.'

Many of the Southampton players were what Chapman described as 'natural footballers'; although they had some training together as a team, they were never taught basic skills, and they flourished.

'No one taught me to track the ball, no one taught me how to take a shot,' she said. 'It was just natural. It was just something that I could do. No one told me how to head the ball. I could just do it naturally – and I know that sounds ever so big-headed!'

Chapman went into management after hanging up her boots. 'I decided I was going to retire [from playing], and I wanted to retire at the top – I didn't want people to say, "She *was* a good player."'

Her management career with Red Star Southampton was short but successful, finishing second in the league and reaching another cup final. 'I'd had enough and I left them at the top, and then that was it for me. I decided I'd run the course and I'd done the best I could and that was it. You've got to remember that I had been playing football all my life. I played well into my thirties. And I just thought, "You know what? You've done it all your life, and maybe now's the time to have some you-time."'

'We went to the cup final and [I] was only the second woman manager to take a team to the cup final. I'd played for England, I'd been a manager at the top, I'd been a footballer at the top and I thought, "I don't have anything left for you." And that was it really.'

A decade later, in 1985, Kerry Davis got the same offer as Chapman, Foreman and Lopez – and like Lopez, she decided to head to Italy to play football semi-professionally. Unlike Lopez, she spent four years out there.

'It was just the chance to play football, that was the appeal,' she explained. 'You didn't have to go to work – you could just play football.'

She was 23 when Lazio spotted her playing for England, and her day job was with the council. She accepted their offer straight away, and moved to Italy, taking up language lessons immediately. She spent a year with Lazio, then moved to Trani in the south of the country on a swap deal with Carolina Morace.

'I thought I was a free agent, but apparently when you signed for an Italian team then there were three pieces of contract and you needed to sign them all – you keep one, one goes to your club, and one goes to the federation,' she explained. 'The piece was not sent to the federation, so to get [me] free from Lazio what they decided to do was a player exchange.'

After two seasons there, and a further year at Napoli, Davis decided to return to England and re-sign for Crewe, where she had spent her teenage years. She had started playing football because she wanted to emulate her older brother, and found a local team, Sandbach, that were happy to take her on when she turned 11.

'A lot of the players I played with, you taught yourself,' she said. 'I watched a hell of a lot of football. Every game that I could watch, I would watch. I grew up playing against boys, men, played a lot of street football, even someone like Wayne Rooney who reads the game well, is extremely intelligent, and he grew up playing in the streets with the kids.

'Tactically a lot of players of my generation were very aware, could read a game, were good footballers ... [but] I wasn't coached until I was probably about 22, 23, and I was coached in Italy.'

In 1991, Karen Farley, a striker for Millwall, was inspired by Davis. Her club coach knew someone in Sweden whose team was short of forwards, following two players suffering cruciate

ligament injuries and, more happily, another going on maternity leave. Farley, just turned 20, went for a trial, which went
well, and she was offered the chance to go out there and play
for Lindsdals.

'It was quite a daunting thing,' she admitted. 'A lot of people
I remember at Millwall were like, "What are you doing? Why
do you want to go over there and play? You don't know anyone.
You don't know the place!"

'I had no idea where I was going. Sweden at that time, it was
like, you know, Björn Borg and ABBA and that was it! I guess
I've always had this thing inside me that was like, "Sod it, if I'm
given an opportunity I'm going to take it. And if I fall flat on my
face and it doesn't work out then I just come home." But it didn't.'

With Sweden yet to join the European Union, she needed a
work permit. 'I've still got my passport from that time, and I've
still got my work permit in my passport that says *Profession:
football player.*' Only the overseas players had the honour of
officially being a professional; Farley was given an apartment
and a small stipend, enough for her to survive on. She stayed
there for two seasons, and following relegation she moved to
Stockholm to play for Hammarby. She began a flexible job as a
cleaner – for a firm run by the husband of a team-mate – and
later got a job with the Foreign Office, working at the British
Embassy, later becoming vice-consul and handling immigra-
tion issues. Farley spent the rest of her playing career in Sweden,
making it her home, and her involvement with the England
squad meant that she had a particularly clear perspective on the
gaps between the standard of football in the two countries at
the time.

'Even the club that I went to first of all, they had lots of
sponsors, and we used to train Monday, Tuesday, Thursday,
Friday . . . play on a Saturday,' she said. 'Sweden is quite a big
country, and we would often have to travel overnight and stay
in hotels, and it was a different world.

'We didn't warm up here in England. We just went out on the pitch and had a little knock around – half the people had a pint before!' She laughed. 'It was crazy. That first week I went, the warm-up, I was like, "Oh my God, are you serious? Have we now got to play a game after that?" So it was just the attention that they put in – your kit, you've got training kit, you've got boots, you got given everything you needed, you had access to a physio when you needed it. I had a cruciate ligament injury out there – there was no question about going on the NHS or something like that, I was taken straight to a private clinic, had the operation, the rehab and everything.

'It was a different world when you compare it to how it was over here [in England]. Some of the pitches that we used to play on over here – it was like cow fields. Over there we were playing in proper arenas, and we had people that used to come and watch us, whereas here it was like your mum, your dad and maybe a bloke that was walking his dog over the park. There, they advertised it, we were in the newspaper every week without fail. I remember walking down the street in this little town and because it was new, it was different, having a foreign person over playing, I was forever getting people coming up asking for autographs. It was quite something for that time – and then when you came back obviously there was very little.'

Lindsdals also needed a defender, and after another phone call back to England, Farley was joined by Wimbledon's Tina Mapes, who also picked up a work visa stamped with her new job title of professional footballer. The pair had known each other for years, growing up in the same area of Kent and playing against each other, but never on the same side. They had the chance to do that for the first time across the continent.

'I had been in and around the national squad, but wasn't breaking through,' recalled Mapes, who had had some success with Millwall Lionesses right at the start of her senior career.

She knew that the people who picked the England team would be unlikely to watch her regularly when she was playing in Sweden, and it did make her pause for thought whether it would be the right decision to emigrate. 'I thought, "Well, if I've got there once, I can get there twice to that level." I believed in myself in that sense, so it was really a no-brainer to me. How many opportunities am I ever going to get to do this? It's in a different country, different way of playing, test yourself completely. So I decided, "Why not go for it?"'

Both Mapes and Farley had year-long contracts at first, and were treated as professionals compared to the local players who were still amateur. The team avoided relegation in that first season, which was viewed as success for a relatively new side, but as the best players – including Farley – were poached by other teams, they disintegrated and dropped down, leaving Mapes stranded.

'I was what, the grand old age of around 21, 22,' she said, 'and thought, "Well, it's not happening any more in that sense over there – come back." I was out of contract, out of visa, so I had really had no choice but to come back from that point of view, just come back into normality really, find a job, start again, find a new team to play for.'

Mapes returned to England and had her pick of teams to play for, and decided to join Croydon, managed by her former Millwall team-mate Debbie Bampton. She also finally made the breakthrough into the national side, playing in the 1995 Women's World Cup.

'I won't say it improved me – I don't think it improved me,' she reflected. 'I was in charge of myself, I was in a foreign country, I had to learn to respect their country and adopt it – really, they adopted me, I adopted them, and I adapted, I think. I think that's a better word than improved. I learnt a new language, took myself to school, to try and learn the language, so, yeah, probably I grew up quite a bit.'

Farley reflected on her time in Sweden with a great deal of fondness, and a touch of amazement when she considered all she had achieved. 'It's quite interesting when you look back now,' she admitted. 'Now I'm a mum of two little children and they look at me sometimes, when they see photos and things, [and say,] "Was that you?" Yeah, that was me!'

EIGHT

THE ENIGMA

IN THE HONOUR ROLL FOR the Women's FA Cup are nestled a handful of rogue teams. They do not share their name with luminaries from the men's game, nor were they adopted by a big parent club in the years after their success.

Lowestoft Ladies, the 1982 winners, are one of them. Goals from Angie Poppy and Linda Curl won them the trophy against Cleveland Spartans on the artificial pitch at QPR's Loftus Road. Six months later, the club folded.

'About a year and a half ago, I was just on Wikipedia,' recalled Ipswich-based journalist Ali Rampling in 2021. 'I was just looking through the list of Women's FA Cup winners, and it had Lowestoft on there, and I'm from Suffolk, so the name rang a bell.

'Lowestoft is not particularly sporty, it's just this tiny little town, so I couldn't believe they had won the FA Cup – this history of women's football I had no idea about. Then I just googled it and there's effectively nothing on Google about them at all, then I found something in the Suffolk library archives about them and it said the team had been forced to disband effectively within months of them winning the cup. So, well, not only did they win the cup, they've got this really sad story that's quite typical of women's football at the time.'

Rampling took it on as an investigative project. The local library archives gave her access to press cuttings, and she decided to drop Lowestoft Town FC a line. Although the women's achievements had been nearly four decades earlier, she was hopeful that perhaps someone might be able to point her in the right direction to find out more. 'With Lowestoft being quite a small place that was quite helpful,' she explained, 'because it's a sort of everyone-knows-everyone sort of thing.'

Rampling made contact with the women's club secretary, and from there began to track down some of the players of that 1982 team to find out why their glory years were over so quickly.

'They were basically a really, really rare club, where they were almost a victim of how successful they were,' she said. 'They were so ahead of their time – they played at Crown Meadow, which is the men's stadium. The men's team let them play at this stadium and then they said they normally got sort of 200, 300 supporters there, which was more than the men's team were getting at the time. They would take a minibus to away games with 20 to 50 supporters. They were just a really professionally run club.'

As teams outside big cities had found when the Women's FA had initially launched, it was difficult to sustain a side. The travel to every single away game was expensive and energy-sapping, and opponents hated having to make the long journey to Suffolk as well. After their own division folded, and with no other leagues willing to take them on, they disbanded.

'Very few other teams were as well supported and financed as Lowestoft,' said Rampling, 'so while Lowestoft could afford to travel to play the teams, not many other teams could afford to travel to this easterly place to get beaten quite heavily!'

Stewart Reynolds, a semi-professional player with Lowestoft Town, had taken on the job of managing the women. He brought in his then-wife Maureen, a strong centre-half, and set about creating a squad to win trophies. Lowestoft had reached the Women's FA Cup final in 1980, losing to Southampton 1-0, but Reynolds thought they had deserved that defeat.

'We were still building our side up,' he pointed out. The 1982 cup run, however, was an entirely different matter.

'I was playing football rather than pushing prams around,' recalled Angie Poppy. 'My brothers played football too so I just joined in with them and that was it from a very young age. There was only one route in and one route out of our estate. It was pretty safe.'

Poppy was good at all sports, representing her school in all of them. Once, she even got to play football for her house. 'The teacher who was in charge of the football team really pursued my case to let me play for my house team – that was the first time any girl had actually represented their house.'

Playing football was her dream, and she wrote to the two big men's clubs in the East Anglia region to ask if they had women's teams. In the early 1970s neither Norwich City nor Ipswich Town had teams of their own, nor could they recommend a local club. She found Middleton Ladies, just four miles down the road from her village of Knodishall, and spent Sunday afternoons playing for them – after Saturdays playing hockey for a women's team and Sunday mornings playing hockey for a mixed side.

Middleton Ladies were not, however, a particularly strong side. In fact, in Poppy's sole season with them, they finished bottom of the league, with a huge goal difference. She wanted to push herself and play at a higher level, and got the chance when her side played Lowestoft and the manager invited her to get in touch if she was interested in transferring. Of course she was, and she joined them when she was 20, travelling 25 miles there and back for home games, and even more for away games. Lowestoft beat all the local sides with such ease it was almost pointless playing them, so they ended up joining a league populated mostly by London teams to get a better standard of competition, but it meant very long journeys every other weekend.

Poppy had to give up playing hockey, but it was not a tough decision for her. 'I always wanted to play football. Always. Always. From the time I was six or seven I always wanted to play football, and I always said, "I'm going to play for England."'

She had no idea that there even was an England team at that point, but in 1976 she got her first call-up to represent her country against Wales at Bedford Town FC's Eyrie ground. She got a lift there from one of Middleton's followers, and joined up with a squad full of players she had never met before, let alone played alongside. They had a couple of training sessions before the match itself and she got to enjoy one of the best moments of her footballing career.

'It is definitely one of the proudest moments, putting that England shirt on,' she explained. Scoring a goal in a 4–0 win in that debut game was also a favourite memory.

For Lowestoft, however, Poppy's greatest triumph was scoring against Cleveland Spartans in the Women's FA Cup final at Loftus Road in 1982.

Winning the Women's FA Cup was one of Vicky Johnson's remaining ambitions in football.

'It is a biggie,' she said. 'That was the one thing that I hadn't done in my career. One of my goals was to win, like most players, a cup winner's medal, so it was a really big deal.'

Johnson was another England international in that Lowestoft team. She had signed for them from Tottenham – one of their few real rivals – a few months previously, moving to East Anglia to be with her partner. 'Spurs were a good team,' she recalled, 'but, see, compared with Lowestoft, they were very average.'

She was used to training hard. Tottenham were ground-breaking in the intensity of their training regime at the time – they had three scheduled sessions a week, with much of it focused on fitness, stamina and running. Lowestoft were similarly organised, although they also expected players to do a lot of training by themselves, considering the amount of travel that was required to get the entire squad together. Bearing in mind that these women were amateurs – Johnson was a social worker in a day centre when in London, later switching to residential care when she moved to Suffolk – it was a big commitment.

The training had a big impact, though; Johnson thought the standard of the league had improved by the time she signed for Lowestoft. They were not necessarily winning by 10 or 15 goals every week, but most weeks they did rack up a win by at least a couple of goals, and the season they won the Women's FA Cup, they were more or less unbeaten in the league as well as their cup competitions. Lowestoft had faced Doncaster Belles in the quarter-finals, coming through a physically gruelling test, then Maidstone in the semi-finals.

'I remember just before I went out to the game, Stewart said to me their manager had said that they didn't think I should play,' said Johnson. 'I think he was trying to wind me up more than anything.'

It was an unusual choice of motivation. Johnson was never the kind of player who needed to prove anything to anyone, and was laid-back and calm. However, Reynolds' words worked; Johnson scored the winning goal, ensuring Lowestoft's place in the final against Cleveland Spartans. They had overcome a mammoth task in their own semi-final, knocking out the mighty Southampton 2–1 in a replay after drawing 1–1 after extra time in the initial encounter. Southampton might have felt something of an entitlement to an FA Cup final appearance; since the competition had been created, they had appeared in all but one of the eleven previous trophy matches, winning eight of them.

Johnson was not bothered about the prospect of playing on the Loftus Road astroturf. As a girl, she had played on artificial pitches in Islington, and knew that all she needed to worry about was assessing the bounce of the ball on the day of the match.

Angie Poppy rather liked the artificial pitch too. 'That was where our pedigree shows, because we were a good passing team, and that was an ideal pitch for us, absolutely ideal,' she said. Getting the chance to play in front of a sizeable crowd was a bonus; because the match was hosted at Loftus Road prior to QPR's home fixture in the Second Division against Bolton Wanderers, the stands began to fill up as the game progressed, and Poppy felt sure that they had seen an impressive spectacle, won by a team who were simply so used to success that they could not countenance defeat.

'I've never been nervous playing football, never, ever nervous,' she said. 'My adrenaline goes, I just want to get out on the pitch. Even when I'm warming up, I don't want to do warm-up, I just want to get out on that pitch and let's get that ball, let's go.

'I'm not a very good loser. I had that winning mentality, and there were so many others in that team, who had that winning mentality – and I never got nervous.'

Stewart Reynolds' memories of the Loftus Road pitch were less positive than his players'. 'Professionals couldn't play on it!' he said. 'It was horrible, it was really horrible. We used to get invited abroad a lot – we played on some plastic pitches over in Sweden, and they were perfect, and they really suited our game. But you couldn't be an inch out on that pitch because it would just bounce and be gone. We trained on it two weeks before, to get them used to it – all the skin was off the girls' legs. I was pretty good friends with Glenn Roeder, who was playing there at the time – he didn't like it and he was a footballing centre-half. We'd have liked to have played on a decent plastic pitch – but I'd tell the keeper to kick it out and it would bounce and nearly disappear in the clouds!'

Plastic pitches were controversial even in the Football League at the time, but the Women's FA and their clubs could not really afford to be too picky; if they were offered a ground, they almost always had to accept it for what it was. Still, a League ground added a certain cachet to the occasion, as did the officiating of a League referee, Danny Vickers of Ilford. Linda Curl opened the scoring in the 26th minute, with a typical goalpoacher's strike, with Angie Poppy doubling the lead just before the hour mark, hitting a spectacular effort from a corner.

Acting as an add-on to a main event of the men's game was nothing new for Lowestoft. They had broken new ground when they had hosted rivals Maidstone at Norwich City's Carrow Road ground in March 1981. That was after the Canaries had played Arsenal, drawing 1–1. Fans and report- ers who might never have watched a women's game in their lives before were suddenly presented with this showpiece event – and many were impressed with what they saw, particularly Poppy's screamer of a strike. Reynolds had a chat with a TV commentator after the match, who told him, 'I don't think anybody will see a better goal this afternoon than that one.'

'It was a good game!' said Vicky Johnson. 'Angie scored a really fantastic goal, top drawer-type goal, great stuff. We had a bit of a crowd and it was quite nice because not many men watched women's football. It was quite nice to get some really good feedback from the crowds and they were cheering you on.'

Of course, there were also those who simply could not get over the novelty factor of seeing women kick a ball. Reynolds also spoke to a QPR supporter, who joked: 'It's the first time I've ever been at a match and fell in love with the left-back!'

*

'We won the WFA Cup on Saturday, right,' said Stewart Reynolds, 'and they said we had to play the League Cup final on the Sunday. We couldn't even really celebrate, the players were all shattered and everything – tired, you know, emotionally as well as physically. And we had to play the League Cup final the next day.'

After their cup triumph, the South East league was restructured. London teams did not want to travel to Suffolk any longer, and there was no local league of an appropriate standard for what Angie Poppy described as 'the best team in the land'. Lowestoft Ladies folded, despite the club's best efforts.

'It really sickened me,' said Stewart Reynolds. Softly spoken, with a gentle Suffolk burr, talking about the way his team had been treated, even more than four decades after the event, was still painful. 'I was in disbelief, because we would have travelled anywhere to be in a good league – we would have gone down to the south coast. We didn't care. I mean, at that time it was costing us £7,000 a year to even survive – we had to do money raising and things like that just to go. But we had to travel every other week, 120-odd miles there and back, whereas teams just had to come to us once a year.'

Reynolds had been trying to deal with all the necessary negotiations and allow his players to concentrate on winning football matches.

'West Ham – they came down one day and they brought Alan Taylor, who scored two goals in the FA Cup final in 1975, and we won 28–0,' Reynolds recalled. 'Then I sat at the meeting, and the league had folded, and people were saying, "You can't let the Women's FA Cup winners dissolve! There's got to be a league for them!" The league we were offered was like Manchester City now going into the Nationwide League.'

That offer came some time after the initial dissolution of Lowestoft's league. Such a drop down was not an option; it would have been even less competitive than their previous remarkable seasons.

'The players had worked so hard to get there, to win the FA Cup, and on top of that game, we'd won all the five-a-sides [close-season friendlies] in the summer . . . basically, at that stage, we were quite unbeatable, I think. We never lost a game that year,' he said, counting off the international players he had in his side, including the then-England captain Debbie Bampton. 'They weren't going to go and play in a league like that – that was pretty poor.'

For several of Reynolds' players, that was exactly what happened. Without her team, Angie Poppy decided to give up playing. She turned out in a couple of fixtures for teams in East Anglia to help out friends, but did not join another side, and then had a baby boy with Reynolds in 1985. The birth was not a straightforward one, and so even if she had considered putting on her boots again after becoming a mother, the injury she had sustained to her back would have put paid to it.

'I do remind him now and again what exactly he'd done to his poor mum!' she laughed. In a delightful turn of events, though, her son Carl also took up football, and played for Lowestoft Town for most of his career – even featuring in an FA Vase Final and getting to play at Wembley, which had been one of his mother's ambitions that she never got to fulfil.

Vicky Johnson knew that there were problems in Lowestoft's future. The players had heard rumours, and they were grateful to manager Reynolds for shielding them from it so they could concentrate on winning. The squad were playing some five-a-side matches in the close season when they were told that their previous league was no longer operational, and there was nowhere else for them to compete.

'There was no other league that would take us on, which was really sad. So it was . . .' Johnson paused. Four decades later, she was reliving the moment, and it remained painful and shocking. She gathered her thoughts. '. . . it was like a punch in the face, but . . . what do you do, because there was nowhere to go. So it was inevitable that that would happen. So it was a very, very sad, sad day for women's football because for such a high-calibre team to just fold, because of a lack of interest . . . I don't know.'

Johnson was still upset that the footballing authorities had not stepped in to help them or come up with some potential solutions. 'You don't let top sides go out of business, you just don't do it,' she said. 'And no matter how the girls were willing to travel – and we all were, we were quite happy because we were so used to travelling, we were quite happy to travel to wherever to play football – no one wanted to entertain us. So the club didn't have a choice really, it was taken out of their hands . . .'

The memory of breaking that news to his players still haunted Reynolds. 'I had to come back to that meeting and say to the players, "Well done on winning the FA Cup – unfortu-nately we've got nowhere to go now,"' he said, adding that there were more than a few tears shed amongst the group. 'I don't know what to say, really. I was speechless at the time and I'm speechless now, and it still hurts. It still hurts.'

Vicky Johnson had achieved one of her great ambitions with Lowestoft, but despite going out on that high, she felt dis-appointed, and that the side could have done so much more given the time and resources.

'If the squad were together in today's setting, they would have been European champions,' she speculated. 'There were quite a few girls that played international level. There were so many more people in that squad, that were on the fringes, that were good enough to do the international scene. It was really sad because they would have gone on to be European champi-ons, no doubt about it whatsoever.'

Johnson fell out of love with football after Lowestoft's closure. She joined the Norwich team set up by captain Maureen Reynolds, but she could not settle there.

'Football for me had literally come to a natural end,' she said. 'I played for a couple of seasons [at Norwich], and it didn't have the same sort of feel, and I felt like at that time it was time for me to maybe hang my boots up.'

She was still only 26.

'I wasn't old by any stretch of the imagination,' she explained, 'but I think family life takes over and career takes over. I was just coming up to 15 when I joined Spurs. I'd been playing and travelling for a good ten years. Where you've got all the training facilities and that's basically your job, it would be different, but to play football [then], you had to pay.'

Stewart Reynolds stopped watching women's football after Lowestoft closed. He continued to work in the men's game, coaching youth teams and scouting in the East Anglia region, but he was too sad and disillusioned to step back into the women's arena. He still had plenty of scorn for the officials involved in the decision-making at the time, who he said had no concerns for Lowestoft as a club or for their players, other than ensuring the Women's FA Cup itself was returned to the authorities.

Despite that, he still had fond memories of the Waves and their achievements in such a short space of time. 'I'm more proud of the players because of what they put in. They trained and they knew they had to train. They were always on time. We tried different things – I was doing overlapping full-backs before the professionals were, and it worked a treat. They listened, and when they listened and put it into action, it was lovely to see, lovely to watch, and that's why we used to get big crowds.

'Without a doubt, we would have got better. I mean, Debbie [Bampton] had only just joined us that season, and we had youngsters coming through, which we liked to use. Of course we wanted to build on that. We wanted to continue.

'We would have got better. We would have got better.'

Linda Curl was the big star of the Lowestoft team, and the one player that Ali Rampling had searched for in vain. One of the younger members of the squad, hanging up her boots after the Waves folded was not an option. She had made her senior England debut five years before Lowestoft had won the Women's FA Cup, and had a formidable reputation as a prolific goalscorer before she turned 20. She continued playing after the sad demise of Lowestoft, winning the Women's FA Cup once again in 1986, and racked up more appearances for England.

'She got 60-odd international caps,' recalled her former manager Reynolds. 'I think she got 21 goals in one game, which I think is still a record, and this was with a team that was nowhere near Lowestoft Ladies' standard.'

'She's one of the few players from the team that has her own Wikipedia page – for Lowestoft that's celebrity in itself really,' noted local girl Rampling with irony.

But that was the extent of Curl's internet presence. It was not an extensive Wikipedia page, either; as with all players of that era, accurate statistics for her appearances and goals were tough to come by. She was not on social media, and once she had retired from playing – according to her Wikipedia page, she last played for England in 1990, but it provided no dates for her club career – she disappeared from the world of football altogether.

'I don't think she distanced herself from her football career, necessarily,' said Rampling, adding that her team-mates remembered Curl as a chatterbox, but one who would not particularly want to trawl over her time in football. 'It's not a shyness thing or anything, I think, it's just, yeah, I don't know – just the past is the past or whatever.'

'I've never been one to want my picture in the paper, or have my face out there,' said Linda Curl. 'I don't do Twitter or anything like that, I don't keep googling things. I think it's good that somebody is recording events, I think that's all great, that things are documented – but I don't necessarily want to be the person out there doing podcasts or whatever they are.

'I'm saying I'm really happy to have a chat. As you can tell, I quite like talking. I'm enthusiastic. However, it's not about me, really – it's about just making sure that things are recorded and then it will all move forward, as everything does, doesn't it? Everything in life moves forward, it don't stay the same.'

Curl had made her views very clear. She simply loved football, and although she had plenty of ambitions during her playing career, she had never been interested in seeking the media limelight. It was apparent, however, that she did feel it was a necessity to tell her stories to give a complete view of what women's football had been like when she was playing, and if a journalist managed to track her down or get in touch, she was happy to spare some time to talk about her memories.

Born and bred in Norwich, a 20-minute walk from the city's football stadium Carrow Road, she grew up a Canaries fan. The youngest of three sisters, Curl wondered whether her father had thought his chance of a child with whom he could share fishing expeditions and sport had disappeared when she was born. Her older sisters were very stereotypically feminine, interested in hobbies and pastimes that had traditionally been reserved for girls, and doubtless they had expected the new baby to be just the same. Linda, however, was a different type of child altogether. As soon as she could walk and kick a ball, she wanted to be playing football, and if she was not playing football, she would be playing outside somewhere else on the estate. On a Saturday night, she was allowed to stay up late – if she could keep awake – to watch *Match of the Day* with her dad. She would kick a ball around with the boys at junior school or in the park, but everything began to change when she was on the verge of her teens and moving up to high school.

'I caused a little bit of a stir, because the teachers had never seen women kicking the ball or girls kicking a football,' she said. 'Obviously I was half reasonable, it was fair to say.'

One of the teachers knew someone who had just set up a women's team called, incredibly, the Norfolk Broads, and teenage Curl began to play alongside and against other women for the very first time. It was a complete culture shock to someone who had spent her entire life playing against boys and men – including her dad.

'He'd come and have a kick around – people on the estate would play football, the boys mainly and me, on a Sunday morning, before everyone went home for their Sunday roast or whatever,' she recalled. 'And Dad and everyone would all be kicking the ball around so when I got to play against women – when you have tackles by 20-year-old blokes when you're 13, and suddenly a tackle from a 20-year-old woman, that's a piece of piss! I just would go on because I'm quicker than you and my dad can tackle harder than that.

'I sound flippant. My background was just growing up on the estate kicking the ball, and being not ostracised at all, totally welcome because I could play – so they didn't say girls can't play football.'

Although Curl and her friends supported their local club Norwich City, she was also a fan of Liverpool because she admired one of their stars, Kevin Keegan. When the local papers first started taking an interest in this little girl who was taking the East Anglian football scene by storm, an amazing opportunity came up.

'They sent a reporter to school,' she recalled, 'and they did a little interview and [had] a photographer – and he was a Scouser and we had a little chat and he did some stuff with the Liverpool men's football team at the time. I went, "Oh, my God, my favourite player is Kevin Keegan."

'Norwich City were playing in the [old] first division [the top flight] in those days, and Liverpool came down, and this photographer said, "I've arranged for you to meet Kevin before the game."

'So I went and did that! Absolutely phenomenal. I met Kevin Keegan, and they took photographs and that happened to be a massive picture on the Monday, front of the *Pink 'Un*, the newspaper, which was a big broadsheet in those days. I didn't know I was going to be in – I suddenly pick my newspaper up, and there I am on the front in a big photo. So I obviously got loads of ribbing for that at school as you can imagine, but that was just great!'

Curl found playing in a women's team very easy. She spent half a season with Norwich, and then moved to Lowestoft Ladies, East Anglia's star team. It meant a 30-mile round trip for Curl just for home games, but the intensive travel schedule was not off-putting to her.

'I think you just get on with your life, don't you?' she suggested. 'You get on with what you're doing at the time. You reflect on things more when you're older because you're just doing it when you're 14, 15, 16. I was just getting out there doing it and I look back and I have some absolute fond memories, but I suppose I was quite fearless at the time. I didn't have any doubts I couldn't do it. I was just like, "Get on and go and play football." Probably now I'd be, "Oh, my God, I've got to do that?"

'You have no fear when you're young. You don't set yourself up to fail because you just get on with it.'

Curl had enjoyed flicking through some of her old scrapbooks and memorabilia in more recent years, looking at press cuttings her father had initially kept for her, and she was very glad he had.

'After a lot of years, your memory fades a little bit, especially when it's repetitive stuff you've done,' she said. 'I played football for nearly 15 years. You can't possibly remember every goal in every game.'

There were a lot of goals to remember as well. Accurate records for women's football in most of the 20th century are scarce, particularly at the domestic level, so there are no reliable figures indicating just how many goals Curl scored for Norwich or for Lowestoft. WFA secretary Pat Gregory's extensive calculations and meticulous record-keeping credit Curl with 29 England goals across a 14-year senior international career that began at a precociously young age. It was England manager Tommy Tranter who spotted the potential of Lowestoft's teenage striker. She went to international trials when she was 14, and was added to the squad to gain some senior experience, making her debut a few months later.

'We never made a penny,' she said wryly. 'We barely got any strip or kit, but at the end of the day it meant so much to pull the shirt on for England.'

At the age of 16, Curl joined the police cadets. 'That's quite a sporty thing to get into,' she said. 'I'd already played for England by then, so I didn't get any "girls can't play football". We used to play football at our cadet training day on a Tuesday – everyone pitched in and they made girls play. None of the girls could play apart from me, so the girls would all be just messing about thinking, "When is this going to finish?"

'And I'd be playing against a load of trainee policemen, all probably like five foot ten, and I was five foot three and a half. And apparently at ten o'clock on a Tuesday morning, the whole county hall, the police headquarters, stopped to watch me play football. I didn't know that, I had no idea. And they had a little County Hall newspaper that came out every month and of course they featured me in it – "Oh, everyone stops at ten on Tuesday to see this little police cadet whizzing rings around all the Old Bill!"'

She had always wanted to join the police, much to her sisters' puzzlement. 'I just always wanted to be a police officer. There was nobody in my family from a police background so that broke the mould a bit for my family – "Right, oh, my God, she's off again, she's random, off piste!" My sisters – one was a secretary, one worked at the theatre, and it was like, "Where the hell did you get the police from?" But it was just something that I really wanted to do.

'I went for a job, had the interviews as you do. There were 200 applicants, and 18 got selected, and I was one of the 18, but I had no concept that I wouldn't get in because you don't have any fear. I just thought, "Well, that's all right, that's what I want to do, that's what I'm going to do," and I think in the interviews that probably came over!'

One of Curl's favourite work duties was policing at Carrow Road, often volunteering for overtime, and invariably as a local officer with a local accent getting placed in one of the home stands. On Sundays, however, she would be playing football herself.

'I used to take all my annual leave to play football, and I didn't mind,' she remembered happily. 'I had to take time off every weekend to play so that I could get picked for the England side so for 12 years I never had a holiday because I literally just played football, and all my annual leave went on playing sport.'

She never moved to a club outside the East of England region, and watched with pleasure and perhaps a little envy her international team-mates move overseas and live and play in another culture.

'I couldn't give up my career to go for it,' she admitted. 'I'd love to have gone for two years, lived in Italy, to play football and learn the language, but they didn't do that in the police in those days. You did 30 years and that was that, so it didn't matter. I still loved my job, I had a very happy life balance of work and sport. Can't grumble.'

The decision to hang up her boots came to Curl earlier than it did to many. She had played 60 times for England, but had only one souvenir cap, because that was how the Women's FA had to operate without the resources to give out memorabilia for every match.

'I didn't even get that until about four years after my debut,' she said. 'That's one thing I was slightly sad about. My dad had come to watch my very first international when I was 15 and he passed away when I was 18, and he never saw my cap, which he would have absolutely loved.

'But, you know, it's just a thing that happened. We just got on with it in those days because you just sacrifice whatever to play for your country, if you were fortunate enough to get selected.'

Fourteen years after her official debut, Curl started to want more. She no longer wanted to give up every weekend, and in her late twenties she was finding it tougher to recover from injuries. She had also realised two of her ambitions – to become England's most capped player, which she was for a brief spell, and to win the Women's FA Cup. Now she had more she wanted to achieve in her policing career, and it seemed like it was no longer possible to combine that with football.

'I wanted to do surveillance work,' she revealed. 'As a local person in Norwich I got a reasonable amount of publicity. Women's football didn't get a lot of publicity, but I got quite a lot because I was in town and I was a police officer – they quite liked that: "We've got an international footballer, let's put that forward a bit." So I had two things in tandem, but then you can't have your face all over your local paper if you want to be on surveillance!'

Curl had often captained her teams and taken training on occasion, but she never wanted to become a coach or take a coaching qualification or even stay involved with football.

'I thought, "I don't want to give every Sunday up any more. I want to go on holiday like other people do,"' she said, and instead took up some other sports, most notably squash, playing for the police's national team. 'I kept sporty but I just left my football boots behind, because I'd perhaps done just about everything that I could, and I'd had such a great time. It couldn't really be bettered anyway and so that's why I fell off the radar.'

She loved her policing career, but it was cut short through serious illness, which was followed by another bout of ill health ten years later – the first time Curl had ever suffered sickness.

'This is why people don't know about my life, because I don't really tell them much,' she said, 'but it's been very varied. And it's been . . . yeah, yeah, certainly not dull, I think it's fair to say.'

When she made her England debut, Linda Curl was the youngest player ever to represent an official England – two months past her 15th birthday. Her first cap came in France – and necessitated her first-ever trip on an aeroplane. The opportunity to travel the world with football was one of the reasons she had never regretted giving up all her annual leave from work to play games.

'With the England team we got to travel, fantastic places – some fantastic countries that I'd probably never [go] to – there was a wonderful tour of Japan when I was 18.'

In 1981, Martin Reagan led his England team to Japan for the Portopia International Ladies' Football Festival, an event organised to coincide with a trade fair marking the completion of an island constructed off the coast of Kobe. There his side were joined by Denmark and Italy as well as the hosts.

'We did go to Japan in 1981 – but that was the foresight of the Japanese FA,' confirmed Pat Gregory, the WFA secretary. 'They approached [us] and said they wanted England to go to Japan and could we recommend two other pre-eminent European sides, because they were reasoning that they wanted the best competition for their new national side.'

Gregory was on the UEFA women's football committee for 14 years, throughout the 1980s, and was part of the group who developed the idea for a women's European Championship. It was not called the European Championship, though.

'It was called the UEFA competition for national representative teams, something like that,' said Gregory.

That was because, with only 16 teams taking part, it involved less than half of UEFA's membership, so could not be an official tournament. Of course, England were part of that initial tournament – which was actually formally called the European Competition for Women's Football. Sixteen teams took part in qualifying between 1982 and 1984, organised in four groups: North, including Sweden, Norway, Finland and Iceland; Great Britain and Northern Ireland, including England, Scotland, Republic of Ireland and Northern Ireland; South, including Italy, France, Switzerland and Portugal; and Central, including Denmark, Netherlands, West Germany and Belgium. Matches lasted only 70 minutes – 35 minutes each way – and used a smaller football than usual, a size four as opposed to the more regular size five.

Sheila Parker, the first-ever England captain, was still playing. The skipper of the side, though, was Carol Thomas.

A Hull native, Thomas, then Carol McCune, began playing football in an organised side at the age of 11 just after the 1966 World Cup – joining a works team and playing alongside women two or three times her age.

'The other women that played, they were really welcoming, there wasn't a problem,' she said. With it being a works team, rather than a grassroots leisure club, there was no training during the week, so Thomas would keep up her skills by playing with the boys at school and with her father and older brother at home. 'I played at school with the boys on the playground, playtime, lunchtime – whenever I could play, I played.'

Thomas got her first England call-up at the age of 19, in 1974, having done well at the recent international trials, for which she had had to travel to the Midlands. She benefited from the support of her employer, a large dairy in the north of England, who were happy to allow her the time off. She made her debut against France at Wimbledon, in South London, and admitted that she was just crossing her fingers and hoping that she would be selected for the next squad. Manager Tommy Tranter was impressed with what he had seen from the teenager from Hull in her first few games.

'We had the home international tournament down in Bedford, where we played Wales, Scotland and Northern Ireland,' said Thomas, 'and on the Friday night before we were due to play Scotland, Tommy took me to one side and said he was making me captain. I was absolutely over the moon. I couldn't believe it, I'd only played five games. I just like to think that he could see something in me.'

She married Alan Thomas in July 1979, with their wedding catching the attention of the local press because rather than heading off on honeymoon the bride was leaving her new husband at home to join up with the England squad. They were going to Italy to play in what the newly minted Mrs Thomas described as a '12-nation international tournament', and she added that as she was neglecting her housewifely duties for at least the next fortnight, her spouse would have to clean and cook for himself until her return.

For his part, Alan mentioned to one of the local journalists: 'I'm just glad I don't have to play against her. She is far too good for me.'

Four teams, including England, qualified for the finals, which took place over a seven-week period in the late spring of 1984. In the two-legged semi-final, England faced Denmark, beating them 2–1 at Crewe's Gresty Road ground thanks to goals from Linda Curl and Liz Deighan, and then winning 1–0 courtesy of a single Debbie Bampton strike in Hjørring. Sweden beat Italy 3–2 in Rome and then 2–1 in Linkoping to ensure their place in the final as well.

The final was also over two legs, and Sweden won their home match thanks to Pia Sundhage's 57th-minute goal in Gothenburg. England had a deficit to overcome when they hosted their opponents at Luton's Kenilworth Road. Linda Curl got that goal back in the first half, but the two sides could not be separated, and with no extra time, it was down to penalties to decide the outcome. Sweden won the shoot-out 4-3 to become the first European champions endorsed by UEFA, even if it was not an 'official' tournament.

It was Thomas who led the side out in Bedfordshire in June 1984 in the pouring rain – conditions that Pat Gregory remembered as 'ghastly'. Thomas admitted that she had thought the match would be called off, with the incessant rain for days previously, but in retrospect she realised that with it being the second leg of two, the governing bodies would have just wanted to get the game on.

'I think Luton was very good to put us up,' said Thomas. 'It was very difficult to play, you just had to try and get it out to the wings if you could. We'd have been better wearing wellies, I think.'

Retrospectively, she was even prouder of what the team had achieved, despite defeat in the final. 'To get to the first-ever European Championships final, for either women or men, was a great achievement,' she said, 'and we had a good squad, Martin had us all sorted. He was a shrewd Yorkshireman, Martin Reagan – he'd got a good squad together and we did our best.

We were just unlucky at Luton, playing on that pitch, but I thoroughly enjoyed it; it was a great achievement, and very proud to be captain of the England team at that time.'

The European final was one of Pat Chapman's career highlights. 'That is one of the medals I actually keep out in the house,' she said.

Her best friend Liz Deighan had somewhat different memories of the day. 'Conditions were awful,' she said. 'It literally rained all day. There's photographs of us playing and all you can see is the mud splashing up. All our kit was absolutely soaked. All the way through we had mud where I don't believe you can really get mud, you were sliding around on your backside. It was awful.'

Deighan had another reason for not wanting to recall the match – she missed a penalty.[1] 'I've blocked it out, really,' she admitted. 'It wasn't a very good penalty really, but bloomin' heck, the ball was awful – you know, you're running and you're just running through water.'

Not long after that day, Luton Town's owners installed an astroturf in place of the grass, thinking that it would open up a number of commercial opportunities – primarily pitch hire, as the wear and tear would not show as it did on grass, where poor drainage led to puddles of water and mud, with sand or sawdust sometimes used to soak it up.

'I would rather have played on a plastic pitch because I used to love five-a-side,' said Deighan ruefully. 'I loved five-a-side, and the speed of five-a-side. I was always small. I was only

---

1 Due to the limited written records kept of the women's game alongside very little media coverage, there is some confusion here. Deighan is adamant about missing a penalty, but the record books say that the two England players who missed in the shoot-out were Linda Curl and Lorraine Hanson.

about seven stone ten when I played, but I was quick, you know, I was quite nippy. So I loved all that speed and being able to run fast and move quickly and change direction quickly. So, on that muddy pitch, it didn't suit my game at all.'

Deighan had been lured to settle in Merseyside from her native North East by a familiar name – Sylvia Gore, who admired her performances for the national team and wanted her to turn out for her Fodens side. So much did Gore want Deighan at her club that she even opened up her home to her, giving her the spare bed at the family home for her first six months in the area. Although the spell at Fodens only lasted for a year, Deighan played a role in revolutionising women's football in the entire area, setting up clubs in Southport, St Helens and then Knowsley, and benefiting from the increased competition and improved standard of play.

'If you're playing with better players, that's bound to bring you on, isn't it? So that helped to increase my chances of staying in the England team,' she said.

Deighan began to coach while she was still playing, and impressed the governing body enough to be asked to take charge of the England junior side, although she was asked to stand aside when the FA took over the running of the women's game. After 20 years of dedicated service to football, she stepped away completely in 1992, worn out with the travel and the demands of working and commuting as well as training and coaching.

'I had 20-odd years of constant football – I didn't have any break,' she said. 'I played all throughout the season, and then I was away with England during the close season, so I had to train all the way through the 12-month period, without stopping. I think I just got a little bit tired, so I just packed it in. But I think in hindsight, I packed it in just a little bit too soon.'

*

Sheila Parker started to consider the possibility of retirement in 1991, but kept going until 1994, hanging up her boots at the age of 46.

'I used to think, "I've had it now,"' she admitted. 'You could see the younger players really flying. I mean I could use the brain and use the ball that way. So you didn't need to run as much . . . but I loved it.'

She treasured the memory of her England career, and the honour of the captaincy, explaining that it made her think: 'I must have been put on this earth for something.'

In the absence of a formal Women's World Cup, but with national teams now well aware that the governing bodies would not permit anything unofficial, an invitational tournament was set up to give some of the women's national teams the chance to compete against each other. The Mundialito was first hosted in 1981, in Japan; and then it took place in 1984, 1985, 1986 and 1988, in Italy every time. In 1985 and 1988, England were the winners, both times beating the hosts in the final.

In 1985, it was still Carol Thomas who wore the England armband. The victory that year made up for the disappointment of the European defeat at Kenilworth Road the year before.

'We certainly made up for it in the Mundialito and for that, for that moment, even though it was unofficial, we were world champions,' said Thomas. 'That was great for me as well as the rest of the girls – it was fabulous.'

Thomas proudly showed off photos on social media of the shiny silverware she had commemorating England's win at the 1985 Mundialito. It was a miniature trophy mounted on a black and white marble plinth, with a plaque engraved 'Mundialito '85 – Winners – Italy 2 England 3' on the left, and the crest of the Women's Football Association on the right. It was clearly a greatly treasured memento of her career, but she was not shy in revealing the darkly funny truth – that the players had each paid to be able to take one of these commemorative trophies home with her.

Kerry Davis – who was one of the younger players in the 1985 squad, aged just 23 – looked back on the Mundialitos with interest, particularly England's first encounters with the USA, which she thought had shaped the next three decades of women's football across the world.

'They came to the Mundialito [in 1985], and that was the first time they'd come to Europe,' she said. 'We beat them 3–1, and we beat them quite comfortably. They were good athletes, technically they were pretty decent, but the first game they played was against Italy. Back in the day the Italians liked pulling shirts, they were quite sly, so when the Americans played against us, they thought, "Oh, that's how the Europeans play," so they decided to use those tactics on us, but we beat them.

'I played against Mia Hamm, she went on to become this superstar, but when you played against her you wouldn't have thought the Americans would have taken off, but they did. They went away and learnt from that and just became what they are today, so, yeah, that tournament was the catalyst of the Americans changing the face of the game, for themselves and for others.'

The 1985 Mundialito was Carol Thomas' favourite memory as an England player, ahead of the UEFA European Championship final. She also had fond memories of the trip the England squad took in 1981 to Japan, despite their comparative lack of success.

'That was the first time I'd ever been that far,' she recalled. 'We flew across and they were really putting money into it. We were welcomed like film stars, to be quite honest. The training facilities, they provided all our kit, and training kit, and everything. Yeah, it was a fabulous experience.'

She stepped back from England duty in September 1985, playing her final game while she was pregnant with her first son.

'I always say Andrew was the first man to play in women's football,' she smiled. She was almost 31 when she had her son, and 33 when she had his brother two years later. 'I concentrated on them both, the family life, basically, and my husband. He supported me a lot and he had given up so much, so I gave a bit back to them.'

Thomas' husband Alan, who had been so complimentary about his new wife's footballing ability in the newspaper articles about their marriage, had continued to help with her training throughout her career. A keen amateur footballer himself, he had met Carol in 1975 at a friend's party, about a year into her England career.

'He was and still is really, really, really proud of my achievements,' she said. When their boys were old enough, the Thomases combined efforts to set up teams for them, and shared coaching responsibilities for a boys' side in a local league.

Kerry Davis had stepped back from football after her retirement from playing. She enjoyed watching her young nephew play for one of the Sheffield Wednesday junior sides, but she no longer played, and she did not coach. In fact, she rarely mentioned her football career.[2]

'Most work colleagues who knew about it were really supportive, but I don't talk about it,' she admitted. 'A guy I work with now said, "Hmm, you played for England, and you never told me!" Even one of my closest friends, I didn't tell him. Every time I talk to him, he goes, "Have you got any more secrets, Kerry?"'

'People I meet now, you get the odd one – "It's only women's football" – but not many of them. I just take no notice of

---

2   Davis was inducted into the National Football Museum Hall of Fame in November 2022.

them – boring. Most people are supportive, and still think I can play! I say, "No, I'm past my sell-by date, I've got dodgy ankles, I haven't played for a long time." Since women's football has come to the forefront more, more people ask, but when I went to watch my nephew, he introduced me to one of the coaches at Sheffield Wednesday, and goes, "This is my auntie Kerry, who played for England." He was like, "Oh, OK."

'We're the forgotten generation.'

NINE

THE BELLES

IN THE 1960S, WOMEN AT football were welcomed if they were happy to slot into some roles. That included selling raffle tickets at half-time; a smiling young woman was more likely to entice male fans to part with their money. Some of the proceeds would go towards prize money; some of it would go towards club funds.

Sheila Stocks was one of the Golden Goals girls at Doncaster Rovers. It was her local club, the one she had supported all her life, and it was a bonus that she got to help them out and watch the matches for free. The more the Golden Goals girls talked, the more they wondered why they did not and could not have a football team of their own. Of course, Rovers did not have one they could join, nor was it a suggestion that would have been entertained.

They set up their own in 1969 and became known as the Belle Vue Belles, after the name of the town's famous sporting arena. At that time, there was little infrastructure to help the Belles get a foothold, so each player bought her own kit, and turned up to training in a local park and a church hall, waiting for the street lights to come on in winter and illuminate the pitch as they had no access to floodlights. They played friend-lies and eventually joined a local league; when that folded they had to travel further afield to play teams in Derbyshire and Nottinghamshire. The Women's FA were established by this point, and the Women's FA Cup meant they also got some fixtures further away, travelling to far-flung parts of the country to play. As they became more established, more players wanted to join an up-and-coming team, seeking success and progression.

The entire Stocks family were integral to the running of the club.

'[Sheila's] mum used to do all the washing of the strips, she did the half-time oranges, when it got cold she used to bring soup in flasks, and her father was there as well – he came to watch,' recalled former player Gill Coultard. 'It was a really tight-knit team.'

Sheila Stocks qualified as a teacher, and married one of her colleagues – a former professional footballer named Paul Edmunds. He joined them for pre-season training in 1984, and was shocked at how poor their drills and fitness were. He took over as first-team coach, and so the family link with the club continued, even when Sheila was no longer an automatic choice in the starting line-up.

Coultard was one of eight children – the youngest, with four brothers and three sisters. Her brothers took her to her first-ever football match, where they watched their local side, Doncaster Rovers, and she fell in love with it instantly. She joined in the kickabouts in their street, with plenty of other families having lots of children, and got to play for the teams when she started school.

Of course, once she went to secondary school at the age of 13 in 1976, she was banned from playing alongside boys. Coultard was not the only girl who suffered from this ruling; famously in 1978, a 12-year-old schoolgirl named Theresa Bennett took the FA to court after being prohibited from turning out for her team Muskham United alongside boys. She won the initial case, but the judgment was overturned on appeal. It was the starting point for an entire review of girls' football, and a reconsideration of when mixed football was appropriate, but it was still two years away when Coultard started at her new school. She was fortunate; her PE teacher told her that there was a women's team in Doncaster that she could join – if she got through the trial. Coultard knew that women's football existed; she had seen a couple of match highlights on television featuring Southampton and QPR, and she was excited to go along to the Belles' training session, at the town's old rugby ground.

'I turned up and I thought, "Wow,"' she said. 'Everybody must have been ten years older than me – probably a little bit older, some of the players, the likes of Sheila – and then I just grasped it, really. I enjoyed it, I went on the Friday and I think the following week I was playing in the first team. We didn't have like they have now, the different centres for different age groups. It was a case of "Right, you're here, you play." So at 13, I've got some pictures somewhere of me sat there, this scrawny little kid sat on the front, and that's how it took off.'

Coultard lived just on the outskirts of the town, and took an eight-mile bus journey from her house to the transport interchange. Then another player from the squad would pick her up from the bus station and drive her to training, and make sure she got her bus back afterwards. She would get home at around quarter past ten in the evening, and then be up on a Saturday morning to play hockey for the school. Perhaps it was fortunate that at that time Belles trained only once a week – on a Friday night, in preparation for the game on Sunday.

Once word got out about this talented 13-year-old, other girls decided they might like to try football as well. The local newspapers were interested in Belles in general and Coultard in particular.

It was not too long before Coultard got an international call-up. She had been linked with representing the Republic of Ireland, which Coultard attributed to her Irish surname, but she always wanted to play for England, to play at Wembley, and to score a goal for her country – and over the years she achieved all three ambitions. Her first call-up, ironically, was to face Ireland in Dublin.

'I'd never flown before, I'd never had a passport – don't forget I'd come from a family of eight and I was the youngest!' she said. 'In those days, my parents were working parents. We didn't have a lot of cash, there were eight of us to be brought up, so it was a bit of panic stations, really. The first thing was: "How do I get a passport?" because none of my family at that point had passports, and then to go on a plane, I just thought, "Oh, my God."'

Alongside Angela Gallimore, Coultard was one of two debutantes in a 16-player squad selected by manager Martin Reagan. She did not start, but came on as a substitute, and immediately after the game was approached by an Irish journalist.

'Somebody came over and wanted to do an interview, and [said], "Do you know you could play for Ireland?" and I went, "Oh, right, no," because I'm oblivious to all this, so he took my address and everything!' she recalled, adding that she did get a letter inviting her to switch allegiance, but she told them she was English and would represent England.

Representing England then was not a massively elaborate affair. Coultard recalled travelling on a Friday, staying over at a hotel on a Saturday night with the squad, playing a match on a Sunday, and being back at home ready for school or work on a Monday.

It was tough for players to keep up their fitness, with few qualified coaches involved in the women's game, and so few opportunities to train together.

'We weren't really coached, were we, to be fair,' said Coultard, looking back on her time at Belles. 'Harry Barton used to do all the ticket sales for Doncaster Rugby League club, and he was our manager, then the more professional one was Paul Edmunds, because he was an ex-footballer, for Leicester City, played in the same team as Gary Lineker, so he'd probably be the one that pointed us to different things, but even then it wasn't coaching as we would call coaching now.'

The first time Coultard encountered properly structured training sessions was in 1995, when the FA took over the England team and appointed Ted Copeland as the new manager. It had taken the FA some time to take women's football under their wing officially. Only an order from FIFA had finally forced their hand, formally folding in the Women's FA to their set-up, and taking charge of the representative national team as well.

'You just used to get together, do your warm-up, and you just played football,' she said, adding that when she watched professionals training years later, they did the same kind of drills as she had done in the later years of her career. 'They just get together, do the warm-up, and they just play football, but it's the tactical side of it that changes. You've got all these bloody video things and they're showing you what you've done wrong, and things like that, that's all they do.

'I went back to sweeper with Ted, and it was just understanding where you need to be if the ball is on that side. I was quite fortunate that I can understand football – not that the other girls couldn't, because they were all football-minded people . . . It was just them little things really, nothing really major changed. The fitness side of it started to change, the way that we had to train. You were training twice a week at your club, it then went up, you had to try to more or less do something every day.'

England missed the inaugural Women's World Cup in 1991. They had failed to qualify. The 1991 UEFA Women's Championship essentially acted as a qualification tournament, and England were knocked out in the second round, losing 6–1 to Germany. However, Coultard was the captain when England ventured to their first-ever Women's World Cup in 1995, the second edition.

'It was a bit gung-ho!' she said. 'We flew to Denmark and then got a boat across to Sweden. You've got other teams in the same hotel, and everything, the Swedes were fantastic, everything got decked out, there were posters everywhere and things like that.'

During Coultard's England years, they played five or six international games a year. It makes her century of caps all the more impressive, 119 England appearances over the course of more than two decades.

'The only person who ever dropped me in my international career was Hope Powell in Norway, which was my last game [a 7–0 defeat in June 2000 in which Coultard was named as substitute],' she said, 'so yeah, never been out injured, I played almost every England game, never missed anything. It's no mean feat to do it that way, but there's lots of people who made a lot more sacrifices than me. I was quite fortunate, I was working, but I had companies that backed me to go away, and if I had any days off they sponsored me through them.'

She vividly remembered the phone call from Powell that ended her career. 'She said, "I think it's time for you, I'm not taking you away, it's time for you to retire." I said, "So what you're saying is basically you're retiring me, because I don't want to retire," and that's what she did.'

An upset Coultard spoke to her former England boss Ted Copeland, with whom she was coaching at the National Women's Football Academy in Durham, who advised her to write to the FA and announce her retirement with immediate effect.

'I packed the Belles in at the same time, because I couldn't play football for Belles – even though I knew I had a couple of years left in me – and not play for England,' she said. 'The two went in hand, because it's been in my blood since I was 13, so that had to happen. That's Hope's decision, there's nothing anybody can do.

'Everybody's career has to come to an end. I was fortunate that my career for 20 years had been fantastic really.'

It had been a career of over two decades in service primarily to Belles. Like several of her peers, Coultard had an offer to play in Sweden at the start of her career, but she felt she was too young for such a big step. Instead, she spent the vast majority of her club playing days with Belles, with a five-year spell at Rowntrees after leaving home in 1981, before returning to her first club and finishing at the end of the 2000/01 season.

'I came back and there were two or three people upset that I came back, because they didn't understand why I went,' she said. 'Things did start to change. You could see people's attitudes change as well, and it were hard going . . . to be honest.'

Those tensions and difficulties in her final Belles seasons were chronicled in the media, with a book plus a fly-on-the-wall BBC documentary. Pete Davies' book *I Lost My Heart to the Belles* followed the squad through the 1994/95 season, while *The Belles* was broadcast on the BBC in January 1995. Belles were no strangers to the press, of course; as the biggest and most successful women's side in the country, some of their Women's FA Cup Finals were televised, and the local media outlets were particularly interested in covering them. That kind of exposure attracted sponsors, which meant they had money coming in to keep them running. At the time that the Belles were garnering so much media attention, their chairman was local businessman Robert Kantecki, owner of a DIY firm, who had agreed to sponsor the team so they could afford to play their Women's FA Cup final against Millwall in 1991. He had been shocked by the amount of sexism the Belles faced, with one headmaster in the area turning down free tickets at the start of the next season because he didn't think women ought to be playing football at all. In the space of those three years, things had started to change just a little.

But the book and the documentary brought the Belles to brand-new audiences. Their earthiness and raucousness may have been a shock to some readers and viewers. Certainly, the television programme shocked the powers-that-were at the FA. Three months after the BBC documentary was aired, the FA secretary Graham Kelly sent a letter to Belles, regretting their involvement in the entire project, and bemoaning the language and behaviour of the individuals within it. The Belles were warned about the possible consequences should such an event be repeated – presumably hinting darkly at fines or possible expulsion from competition. It was an ironic piece of correspondence seeing as when they received it, Belles were waiting for the FA to rearrange three postponed fixtures, and Davies quoted an angry Paul Edmunds saying that they should not have been scolded, they ought to have been thanked for raising the profile of women's football.

Davies did not sanitise his book, either; he gave an honest and affectionate appraisal of the players and the club. He wrote about one player quipping that the only training she had done in three weeks out injured was running down the shop to get her cigarettes, and included a post-match mention of one Belles player smoking marijuana with an opponent from Arsenal after one match – although he did refrain from naming either. (He mentioned in one chapter that a feature he had written for a broadsheet newspaper, with a similar tone to the book, had got one Belles player scolded by her international manager and dropped from the squad along with dark mutterings of the crime of 'bringing the game into disrepute'.) The coverage did, however, show the reality of life at the top level of women's football at that time, with the book in particular not shying away from the lack of support they got in terms of fans and finances. The narrative was peppered with some stark numbers as well, with an estimated 12,000 women playing football in England – this was presumably considered a large number by

Nettie Honeyball. © steeve-xfoto/Alamy

The Preston Ladies Football Club – formerly known as Dick, Kerr Ladies –
in 1939. Lily Parr is on the left, with arm extended. © Fox Photos/Hutton Archive

AGOSTO

MEXICO 71

64 PAGINAS ILUSTRADAS   EJEMPLAR DE COLECCIÓN $ 15.00

programa
oficial
para el II
campeonato
mundial
de futbol
femenil

historia del
futbol femenil
en méxico

xochitl

Chris Lockwood's programme from the
Mexico World Cup. © Chris Lockwood

Sheila Parker with the ground-breaking first official England squad. Wendy Owen is in the back row, with the long blonde hair, just behind the skipper's head! Back row (left to right): Lynda Hale, Maggie Pearce (née Kirkland), Julia Brunton (née Manning), Paddy McGroarty (slightly hidden), Wendy Owen, Eileen Foreman, Jean Wilson (slightly hidden), Sue Whyatt. Front row (left to right): Jeannie Allott, Janet Bagguley, Sylvia Gore, Sandra Graham. Not seen in the photo are Sue Buckett and Pat Davies. © R. Taylor/Alamy

Wendy Owen's England sweatshirt from the home international tournament in 1976. © Wendy Owen

Gill Coultard. © Tom Shaw/Getty Images

Angie Poppy's England memorabilia.
© Angie Poppy

Liz Deighan's England cap. © Liz Deighan

Karen Walker playing for England against Scotland in 2001. © Barry Coombs/Alamy

Karen Farley's personal sports bar, displaying all her memorabilia. © Karen Farley

Carol Thomas surprised by Baroness Sue Campbell in 2021 with her
induction into the National Football Museum Hall of Fame. © Ed Sykes/Alamy

Faye White in action for Arsenal. © TGSPHOTO/Alamy

Anita Asante, playing for Aston Villa. © Alex Livesey/Getty Images

Davies, but was minuscule compared to the numbers of men playing recreationally.

Davies, an experienced football writer, opened his book with an overview of the squad, its personalities and its dynamics, emphasising how it was just like any other team, before reiterating what he seemed to see as the strangeness and uniqueness of women being both such dedicated, skilful footballers and often such fun-loving rabble-rousers. Nevertheless, he found himself straying into clichés about typically feminine appearance and behaviour, describing players as 'pertly pretty', 'drop-dead pretty', 'fetchingly pretty' and 'strikingly attractive', mentioning one's 'gorgeous eyes' and going into some detail about what he perceived as one woman's 'sensuality' and interest in sex. Playing devil's advocate, he suggested at one point that female footballers could be accused of defensive naivety (an accusation that was brushed off in his documented conversation with male professional Mark Bright). There were also plenty of stereotypical indicators of the working-class, short-of-money backgrounds the players came from; Davies hinted that the majority of the squad were not interested in books or broadsheet newspapers, but might flick through a tabloid or watch Sky, if they could afford it. There were some suggestions of danger and violence; Davies mentioned one player's doormat being turned over so that the bloodstains on one side did not show, plus her fear of debt collectors finding her, and another having her car repeatedly stolen. There were several dark and disturbing hints about traumatic events in players' pasts, from childhood neglect to sexual assault and domestic abuse. There was even one incident at another club where there had been a punch-up between players on the team bus after a defeat.

Davies likened Coultard to multiple male superstars – Bryan Robson for her captaincy, Diego Maradona for her low centre of gravity. Her natural authority on the pitch went hand in hand with her position as player representative to the club committee, and Davies portrayed her as a role model to the others. He also hinted that she was not a sociable character, and was more reserved than the rest of her team-mates; the phrase he used was 'a stay-at-home square'. He also narrated her understandable concerns that the fly-on-the-wall documentary might damage her reputation as England captain and chances of selection for the 1995 Women's World Cup.

Ironically, Coultard found the writer following the team around for his book more intrusive than the TV cameras. After she lost the England captaincy in 1995 to Debbie Bampton – which manager Copeland had explained as being for her own good – she was unsurprisingly upset, and her negative attitudes triggered squabbles amongst the squad. Davies was on the spot to chronicle it, starting with an argument between Coultard and goalkeeper Debbie Biggins after a 4–1 win over Southampton – the skipper demanded more commitment from the squad, many of whom had been absent from training, while the young keeper pointed out that Coultard herself had missed more than one session in recent weeks. An angry Coultard announced her intention to sign for Belles' rivals Liverpool.

Coultard acknowledged at the time that she had found the season a tough one, with an uncertain work situation not helping her psychological state, and all these factors combining to affect her health and fitness. She knew she had not been a good captain for Belles that year, and admitted it had been hard to motivate herself after all the drama with England.

Looking back on spending a season with a writer cataloguing their conversations as well as their matches, she now thought that each of the squad had probably censored themselves in some situations, knowing they were being watched, but conversely sometimes the omnipresent observer's interpretation of events made them look much worse than they were.

'Sometimes you couldn't be the person you wanted to be, and say what you think, or thought of, without thinking about what you're going to say,' she explained. 'We were in a club where you'd just say what you thought; it didn't matter, people didn't take offence. It's not like today when you've got to be politically correct.

'It was like if he'd bugged your room – does that make sense?

'[It was] great for the Belles to have a book written for them, but I just think there's quite a bit in there that was a generalisation of [the way things were] ... Once you get talking to a reporter you get carried away, and you think, "Should I have said that?"'

Karen Walker was one of the biggest stars of women's football in the 1980s and 1990s. Lean, pacy and with an unerring eye for goal combined with a deadly shot, she tormented defences as she fired Belles to many trophies and led the line for England.

One of her early mentors had observed that her strengths simply could not be coached into a player.

'I knew I wasn't, say, as skilful as everyone else, but I knew how to score goals, I knew the place to be in, and he always used to say to me I had something you couldn't teach,' she said. 'I was a good example of it: doesn't matter that you've not had that coaching, you can just do it at the highest level, and thankfully I did.'

She was also one of the stars of the documentary and the book, and had made it clear to Pete Davies that she was not at all bothered about the consternation it might cause at the FA. In fact, Davies' book suggested that Walker was well aware of the reaction that would be triggered at the FA and within the England set-up by a bird's eye view of the Belles, aired on national television. However, Walker was unperturbed by the chance of a wave of negativity towards her or her team; she played football because she loved it, and she played football with her friends. Her motivation was not to win trophies, but to make memories. Even when she was injured, she was adamant she still wanted to show up at training.

Less rowdy than some of her team-mates, Walker was working in the income support team at the then-Department of Social Security in Rotherham, South Yorkshire, as she had been for the previous seven years, since she was 18; and the television cameras followed her to work there, and back to her domestic life. Her team-mates would hail her goalscoring exploits with bursts of song, declaring that they were walking in a Walker wonderland.

Davies' book characterised her as a more thoughtful, gentle person than some of her team-mates, with a tendency to pre-match nerves, forcing a desperate toilet break in the minutes before heading out on to the pitch for kick-off. The Walker portrayed in his book, however, was not without some rough edges; he mentioned that she would have a kickabout with anybody, including a group of teenage lads, who clubbed together to buy her some cider as a thank-you gift. She was a woman of a thousand small kindnesses: her words of support and guidance for young players, but also her empathy for the people she worked with who were scared or angry because of their unemployment and urgent need for money. It was evident that Walker appreciated her good fortune, much of which had stemmed from football; she was very well aware that had she not had the chance to express herself on the pitch, her life may have gone in a very different direction.

Walker also told Davies about her fitness regime; with Belles training only once a week, she took herself out for a run on three evenings, and on Tuesday nights she did weights in the spare room of the house she shared with her then-boyfriend Dean. Tall and strong, with short blonde hair, Walker also displayed a great deal of reflection and thoughtfulness, particularly when it came to the historic problems that beset the women's game; she argued convincingly that comparing women's sport to men's was fruitless, and instead women's sport should be enjoyed in its own right. (She also made a salient and brave point – arguably 30 years ahead of her time – that much of the excitement around men's football stemmed from the tribalism of the crowd and the subsequent hype.)

Unlike Coultard, she rather enjoyed the spotlight she got as it reminded her of her happy times with Belles. 'It weren't as serious as what it is now,' she recalled. 'They were the most amazing group of people. We just had the best team spirit, absolutely fantastic. And whether we won, lost or drew, we enjoyed it, and that's all I can remember. So I wouldn't swap one second of it – it was absolutely fantastic. I can't remember everything that happened in the documentary, but, you know, I can't remember having any regrets or anything like that. It was an amazing time, and I've just got good memories about it.'

Perhaps Walker's more ambivalent approach to the impact of the media coverage could be explained by the overarching narrative of Davies' book; Belles were mounting a title challenge in an injury-hit season and remained within touching distance of the title until they lost Walker to a knee problem. Manager Edmunds seemed almost relieved when it was no longer mathematically possible for them to become champions, saying that while Walker was in the side, there was always a chance, but without her, there was no hope at all.

Walker had burst on to the scene as a 16-year-old, having never played organised football before. Her entire playing experience had been with her brother and his friends in the park, and she had no idea about women's teams, and had never heard of the Belles. Then her neighbour Karen Skillcorn joined the team and suggested she come along.

'I turned up as a cocky 16-year-old, thinking, "Yeah, I'll have a go, I play with the lads, I'll take them on" – it was just shocking, the difference, but within a year I was in the England squad, so I think it was just right place, right time!' she explained. 'I didn't even know lasses played. So to suddenly see them at that level was massive for me.'

Nobody quite knows exactly how many goals Walker scored for Belles. There were no official accurate records kept for all the games she played, and she was never the kind of person to note down all her achievements. There was plenty of folklore handed down, though; people remembered the season she scored a hat-trick in every round of the Women's FA Cup, and the seasons where she went through spells of averaging two goals per game.

'When I first joined I would come on at half-time and I would score five in the second half,' she confirmed. 'So, at that time, we were that good, we would just used to batter teams so you can't really remember. The only stats I've ever remembered over the years is my England stuff – I can remember most goals and most games that I played for England, that was just different again, but not for club. We just played that many games and that many competitions, I can't remember.'

Walker's international record was also impressive. Called into the national squad a year after making her Belles debut, she scored with her first-ever kick of a ball in an England shirt. It was against Italy in the 1988 Mundialito, and she had been told by manager Martin Reagan that she would only be with the squad to gain some experience. An injury meant that she was called into action in the very first game.

'When the girl got injured, he shouted at me to go on,' she remembered. 'I were that nervous, I could have fainted, and then I literally went on and scored with my first kick. So then I thought, "That's quite easy, isn't it? All right, this lark, isn't it?"

'I thought, "I don't mind coming away to Italy for three weeks, I quite like this!" It weren't a bad tournament for my first real competitive game.'

Walker mentioned in Davies' book that she was not entirely happy with the atmosphere in the England camp under Ted

Copeland's management after Reagan's departure, although she would never turn down an international call-up. She found it straightforward to get time off from the DSS, and felt sorry for her team-mates whose employers were not so flexible or in a position to grant requested leave. The support she got from her work meant she stayed there for her entire playing career, and did not have the chance to pursue her dream job until after she hung up her boots.

'I'd wanted to go in the police since I was quite young,' she said. 'But once I got into the England team I couldn't afford to leave [the DSS], and to then go into the many weeks of training that you would need [to begin a job in the police] and not necessarily getting the time off [for football] because you're in training, so I left it, and left it, and left it, and then as soon as I got to the point where I retired, I applied to the police, and got in. It just worked out.'

Chantel Woodhead was one of the players Davies relied on for comic relief in his book. One of the younger members of the squad, she was portrayed as slightly vague and ditzy, which to a discerning reader might raise questions about how she managed to be so successful at her job in the ticket and sales department of Leeds United.

'It totally wasn't a reflection on how I am,' she confirmed. 'I don't quite know how that come about, apart from I was really laid-back as a character. I would turn up for a game, and it didn't matter to me the opposition, it didn't matter to me in any way, I'm just playing, and whether it was Arsenal or a lower league, it didn't matter.

'So I'd turn up, and I'd be like, "Who are we playing today?" And they'd go, "Channy! It's flippin' Arsenal!"'

'It just was very much of a big wind-up team, really . . . they used to take the mickey out of each other quite a lot. Quite a few of us took a little bit of individual stick, but to be honest, it just went over my head. I knew that wasn't me. To be honest, I was quite a private person. So people didn't really know me . . . I didn't really hang around with the team and after the match I'd take myself home. So there was an air of curiosity, I think, so I just put that around me like that was my character and I let them run with it.

'Actually I was very, very switched on, very, very reflective and very much a watcher. So I saw everything and just took it all in, with a smile on my face. [It was] very much an underestimation but [it] didn't bother me that . . . it went like that.'

Woodhead was one of the rising stars of English football at the time, and had been called up to the senior national squad under Copeland. Like Walker, she was not happy with the way the camps ran, and she was disciplined for one of the most peculiar off-the-field offences in the history of football, which she still thought had stopped her from being part of the 1995 Women's World Cup squad.

'I got dropped for England for wearing the wrong trousers,' she confirmed, referring to an incident during her time with the national team in January 1995, prior to a 1–1 draw with Italy in Florence, when she was substituted at half-time, having been formally warned previously for her non-regulation issue clothes. 'To be honest, [it] still pees me off 27 years later, because I got dropped for the World Cup.'

Woodhead was still evidently angry about the entire incident. It had been suggested to her that her lack of adherence to the strict dress code was a symptom of a lackadaisical attitude, and she refuted that completely.

'I was hardworking, I turned up, I put everything into it,' she said. 'And to say that my dress code reflected my attitude was absolutely disgraceful, and obviously would never ever happen in this day, that somebody will be sent a letter from the FA to say that they've been dropped for wearing the wrong trousers. I laugh tongue-in-cheek now but, you know, really, it's poor.'

Woodhead, like all her peers, had made plenty of sacrifices to play football. Even though she was employed by a professional football club, they still asked her to use her holiday entitlement to go on international camps. She would argue against it by pointing to Leeds' star midfielder Gordon Strachan, the Scotland international, who used to get free pairs of boots for her thanks to his own contacts as one of the most celebrated footballers in the country.

'I'd say, "Well, Gordon is playing for Scotland next week, and he don't have to take his holidays. So if he's an employee and I'm an employee, what's the difference? Why am I taking my holidays? Why can't I be given time off to go and play for my country?" That's how it was: we wasn't seen as important, [or] the same [as the men].'

Playing for Belles and England also required additional training, including a heart-rate monitor sent from the FA to check the necessary activities were being done, with perhaps one rest day a week in the schedule. Bearing in mind the players were not professional and were earning their living wage elsewhere, it effectively meant they were doing their full day's work, then a full evening's training.

'You were working hard,' emphasised Woodhead. 'You were working a nine-to-five job and then you were jumping in the car.'

It was all even more time-consuming if Belles were playing an away match. Woodhead was not fond of staying overnight before a game, or for even longer if it was an international camp.

'I was quite a home girl, really,' she admitted. 'I just liked to play the match and then come home . . . We were only amateurs, so to go [away from] a Friday to Monday was a big ask. All I really wanted was a Sunday dinner when I finished, with my family.'

She gave up playing football just before turning 30, which she thought in retrospect was too early, but the lack of international recognition following her disciplinary breach had hit her hard.

'Since I wasn't going to play for England – and I knew that – ever again, I went off the boil a bit,' she said. 'I played on for a little while after that but then I just had enough. I fell out of love with the game . . . I just quit and I walked away from it. I could have gone on, probably, for another three or four seasons, to be fair . . . but mentally I wasn't there because it was hurtful . . . The ultimate is to play for your country, so what am I playing for, if that's not the goal? It was disappointing.

'I had a good career, I managed to win every medal there is in the game that was available to me, played for my country as well, so I have no regrets. I came out with my knees intact, no major injuries, so I'm thankful for that.'

The pain of the way her England career had effectively ended, though, still rankled, and she remembered the sting very vividly. 'When I got that letter [from the FA], my whole world fell apart. I didn't know what to do . . . I had to pick myself up from it, and, obviously, be stronger from it. I'm a big believer in fate, you know, and things happen to you for a reason. So it obviously wasn't meant to be and I was meant to be somewhere else. Your journey is set for you.'

Gill Coultard finally hung up her boots in 2001. She never signed for Liverpool. Walker continued playing for a little longer, leaving Belles in 2004 to switch across Yorkshire and join Leeds United. Belles were never the same force after that. They won no more league titles, and though they have reached two more FA Cup finals, in 2000 and 2002, they won neither. Still, they retained some ambition, turning semi-professional after that second FA Cup final defeat thanks to a sponsorship deal injecting some cash into the club. Even then, though, club executives confessed publicly that professionalism was a long way away. They spent some years after the turn of the millennium folded into the men's club, Doncaster Rovers, and taking on their name, but switched back to independence when they became founder members of the semi-professional FA Women's Super League (WSL) on its launch in 2011.

Rebecca Hall was one of the players who represented Doncaster Belles for their first-ever season in the WSL. Versatile and speedy, she was one of the brightest talents in the England youth set-up, studying and training at the elite Loughborough Player Development Centre, and signing for Doncaster from Birmingham City.

'I wanted something a bit more for myself,' she said. 'At that point, it was looking ahead. WSL had been mentioned. Birmingham weren't having the backing of the men's team and there was no guarantees that Birmingham were going to be getting a team into the WSL.'

Her friend Nicola Hobbs, the Belles goalkeeper, asked her whether she might be interested in moving, and six months later Doncaster approached her to sign for them ready for the launch of the WSL. Playing for Belles was like nothing Hall had experienced before, because they still had good links with Rovers, enabling them to take advantage of some of their facilities.

'Donny were great with us,' she said. 'They've got a training pitch that a couple of the reserve teams use, and that used to be our home pitch, but once we got into WSL all of our games were in the ground [the Keepmoat Stadium] which was absolutely amazing – that we had the best facilities in the league, because we had. We had that pitch, we had that stadium, we had better changing rooms than everybody else. So we were quite privileged.'

Still, as a semi-professional player, Hall was working a part-time job, in a company running football coaching courses, and finishing off her university degree – and she also had a small child. Balancing that with travelling up to Doncaster from the Midlands three times a week was draining. There was no relegation from the WSL in its first season, and there were plenty of competitive matches; the rules governing the competition meant that the England stars were spread out between teams rather than one club snaffling all the best players.

'The problem we had was we didn't recruit any of those England players!' said Hall with a half-smile. 'I remember when we played Lincoln on the first game of the season – the week before that, Casey Stoney had moved from Chelsea to Lincoln. Well, the season before, there was no way the England captain would have been playing for Lincoln.

'But there were certain clubs that seemed to have a bit more money to spend. Unfortunately we weren't one of those clubs.'

Rather than signing any of the England stars, Belles looked further afield, signing internationals from Ireland, Scotland, Sweden and Canada, and relying on young talent.

'We went down a slightly different approach, so we were always going to be battling in the bottom half of the table,' explained Hall. 'We just needed to be better than a couple of other teams. We beat Lincoln on the first game of the season. We beat Liverpool as well later on in the season and we ended up surviving comfortably, but we were only ever going to survive, we weren't ever going to challenge. It was competitive – we didn't get battered in any games, but we didn't win many either.'

Hall left Belles after that first season. The travelling was too much for her, but there were no more local options for her to stay in the WSL, meaning she went back to her hometown club Wolves, three leagues below.

'I felt like I had more to offer and obviously I didn't want to again play in a team that was battling relegation, and fighting that all the time – that wasn't my game,' she said. 'My game is all about being on the ball, and if you're playing in a team that are fighting at the bottom of the league, chances are you're not getting the ball very much. So I made that decision for myself. I ended up getting made redundant so I had to go and find what I consider a real job. It was all too much to fit in with football, travelling three times a week up to Doncaster – my son was getting older, and I had to make the decision at that point, which is why I then went back and just played local football.'

It was a very different atmosphere after the hype and increased spotlight of the WSL. 'Just the whole kind of aura around it . . . you'd turn up for games and you felt like, "Oh my God, this is amazing,"' she remembered. 'The games were on telly – games had never been on telly before, only like the FA Cup final!

'One game, we played Everton live on BT Sport, and my son was mascot. You turned up to games and you'd get off the coach at an away game or you'd turn up at the ground for a home game and fans were already waiting and it was just absolutely mental. It wasn't something I'd ever seen or I thought I'd ever see in my football career. It was mad. It was really, really mad.'

When Jody Handley was a little girl, her father would put women's football on the television for her. With the Women's FA Cup aired every year, quite often one of the teams in action was Doncaster Belles. Young Handley enjoyed watching the games, but did not realise there was a whole league and pyramid structure for women who played football. She joined Wolves Women as a teenager, and suddenly her eyes were opened. A few years later, she signed for Belles and was called up to the England squad, and was playing for club and country alongside one of the players she had loved watching as a child.

'Kaz [Walker] was always my favourite player when I used to watch it!' she revealed. 'She's such a lovely girl and I've got so much time for Kaz. She's such a positive person and such a great laugh around the camp. She just had everything.'

But Walker and the other Belles were not Handley's role models. 'I was never going to be like them – they probably weren't put on a pedestal, by any stretch of the imagination,' she said. 'I probably still wanted to be like, I don't know, Gary Lineker or someone like that, with that kind of stature.'

Although Handley first signed for the Belles at the start of the 21st century, the atmosphere was just the same as it had been three decades before. Belles were still true to their amateur independent ethos – a huge contrast to what was going on elsewhere as league rivals Fulham were investing money and offering some of their players the chance to turn professional. Handley did not think that Belles' old-fashioned traditions were a bad thing.

'It's built on goodwill,' she said. 'It is the community's club. They haven't got the financial backing. Everything they've achieved is based on their reputation, and how successful they were in the '80s and things like that, and that's what makes it special.'

But she found it a struggle to commute to Doncaster. Having spent time at both Liverpool and Everton, she was still based on Merseyside, and travelling to training took up plenty of time as well as strain. Handley returned to Everton for another decade after that stint at Belles, but found herself back in Doncaster for what turned out to be the last months of her career.

'I didn't get offered a new contract with Everton, and I was a bit bitter and twisted about it at the time,' she recalled. 'I just felt like I deserved one. I just felt like I'd been around for years. I felt like I still had a lot to offer and I just thought as a reward really for being quite loyal and successful in the past, I felt like

I deserved it, rightly or wrongly. So I felt like I still had something to . . . offer in the league.

'Then I went back to Donny and then, obviously, my body had other ideas.'

Handley kept suffering muscle injuries, and every single journey to Doncaster was just to receive treatment or join in a very limited training session. She was training to be a physiotherapist herself, and found herself more and more exhausted by the effort of such an extensive commute. The facilities on offer were fairly similar to the ones they had access to more than ten years previously, while the rest of the women's game had started to move on.

'It's just a hell of a lot of effort – not that I wanted any money or anything like that, but maybe just the quality of things; it felt like it was going back in time a little bit,' she said.

It did not help with her recovery from the recurring injuries. 'I was so frustrated – I'd rehab, I'd do all the right things, take my time over it; there was just no logic to the injuries that were happening,' she said. 'I think it was generally just old age and wear and tear.

'I'd forgotten really how difficult it was to travel to work, to train, to get fit and to compete. I felt like I still had games in me and I still was a quality player and had a lot to give. I just fell out of love with it, really. I think spending a few months at Doncaster, just grafting to try and get myself fit, I just thought, "If I'm having doubts now, then I probably haven't got much longer than like a season left in me anyway. What's the point of just doing it for a point to prove rather than bowing out, not on a high, but on my own terms?"'

At the point when Handley was ready to retire, Belles were in the newly created second tier of the Women's Super League. With clubs awarded places according to their application for licences, Belles had been moved into WSL2 at the start of the 2014 season. They won promotion back to the WSL in 2015, and announced plans for what they called Project Phoenix, which included salaried players and a new training ground.

Belles were relegated back to WSL2 the following year, and although they won the championship again, they opted not to stay in the WSL set-up. Without a wealthy benefactor or a rich club from the men's game willing to subsidise them, it was too expensive to meet the demands that were being placed upon them. Instead, they chose to move down to the third tier, the FA Women's National League, which was still resolutely amateur.

It was clear to Hall then how Belles' future would pan out.

'Doncaster Belles were world-known,' she said. 'Everybody knows who they were in women's football, whereas now – now they're petering out, down into local leagues. It's just such a shame because it wasn't that long ago we were playing at the Keepmoat. In the last game of the inaugural WSL season, we played Birmingham, and Birmingham had to beat us to win the league and I scored a last-minute free kick and we drew the game 2–2, and Arsenal ended up winning the league. We were down the bottom, they were at the top. They had lots of money, they recruited a lot of players, they had Rachel Williams, Jade Moore, Emily Westwood, Karen Carney, Jo Potter, and we drew with them on the last game of the season to stop them winning the league.

'And it's unfortunate that it does come down to money.'

'They're never going to be able to compete, really, until they've got a massive backing of finances from whatever source that they can get,' reflected Handley. 'And it is a shame, because they are who everyone talks about when you talk about women's football, really. I mean, there's still people involved there now who, you know, [have] been involved for like years and years and years, and who played for them.'

*

Hall had what she described as 'the young person equivalent of a knee replacement' requiring a four-year break from playing.

'That's how long it took to recover from the operation,' she said. 'I've had like horse fibre implanted in the knee and all sorts of things, so that plugged the gap that I had, where I had no cartilage in my knee. Then that overgrew.'

Dealing with such a serious knee problem in her twenties ultimately came as no surprise to her. She vividly remembered falling heavily on her knees as a 15-year-old playing for Wolves against Stockport, resulting in so much fluid on the knee that the swelling could be moved around. A fortnight later, she fell on it again, and the fluid disappeared.

'My game was all about sprinting, so I didn't do a lot of the endurance stuff,' she said. 'It's always about power, so it's a lot of stress through your joints. I think it was just years and years of playing, years and years of training. I'd trained every day since I was 12, and it eventually caught up with me.'

During pre-season with Wolves, at the end of a match against Aston Villa, Hall's legs gave way at the final whistle. 'My legs just went from underneath me, and I was like, "Right, obviously that's not good." I just thought it was because my legs were so tired – and my knee was never the same.'

The surgeons initially thought she was showing all the signs of a typical torn meniscus and said she did not need to have a scan but could proceed to surgery.

'It was only when they got into my knee they were like, "This isn't your meniscus. This is a big problem."'

The surgeon was not able to perform the required operation – an osteochondral graft – and said that there was only one person in the entire area who would be able to do it. Hall was sent across to Stoke, progressing through the usual lengthy NHS waiting list with no preferential treatment; as she was no longer a semi-professional footballer her livelihood was not officially being affected.

'I didn't play for a long, long time. Then I always said to my wife, "If my knee's fixed before I'm 30, I'll go and play again, just play at local level."'

Hall was 29 and a half when she recovered from her final knee operation; she had been told she might not even be able to run again, let alone play football.

'I had that in my head all the time,' she said. 'I was like, "Nah, you're not making this decision for me." I was looking on Facebook and people were retiring left, right and centre. That was their choice. I found that so frustrating – you got to go out on your own terms and I didn't. And that was all the motivation I needed then; I knew I still had enough to give.'

Hall joined a local team in the county league to see how she got on. It was just like old times; the team won the league, and she was named the player of the year. More than that, she was the top goalscorer – not bad for someone who was now coming out of the centre of midfield rather than playing any further forward.

'I've completely changed my game at this point because I no longer had the pace, I hadn't played for so long, but also my joints can't hack it,' she agreed. It was also much more convenient for her; her son – a baby when Hall was called up to represent England at the Under-20 Women's World Cup – was now playing football himself, and his own fixture list needed to be taken into account because she was the team's manager.

'His friends literally think I'm the coolest person ever because I'm the only mum that will join in and play with them,' she grinned. 'They're all like, "Becky, did you really play for England?" "Yes, mate!"'

Even with the injuries, Hall thought she could probably still cope with playing at a higher level, but the time commitment was just not possible.

'I know I've still got a lot to offer – in my head I think I could still play WSL,' she said.

Handley left Belles and retired in 2015, aged 36. Since then, she had played in the occasional charity match, but did not miss the relentless grind of semi-professional football, which had been her life for over 20 years. Instead, she was enjoying the nine-to-five routine of working as a rotational physiotherapist in the National Health Service, with the occasional weekend on the schedule. She had qualified with the support of the Professional Footballers' Association, to whom she credited her career.

'People say, "Do you not want to get back into football?" and I think I would love to get back into that team environment and have the facilities and all that kind of stuff, but I just couldn't imagine spending all of my nights and all of my weekends and all of my spare time just with a team and just travelling,' she said. 'I mean, the commitment – I never appreciated it really until I finished, how big a commitment it was, and it still is, it still is. Although now, you know, as a job,' she added wryly, 'it's a lovely job to have, isn't it?'

Handley had been in teams with players who had reaped the benefits of the WSL, both financially and in terms of their footballing development. Nevertheless, she dismissed any idea that she felt envious of those able to play professionally and make a decent living from it.

'At the end of the day I've lifted the FA Cup, I've played in a World Cup, and nobody could take that away from me. I know it's very morbid, but when we're all lying on our deathbed, all you've got is memories, and I've got as good memories as anyone in the game now.

'I'd like to have known how good I could have been playing every day. It's frustrating for me because although I played for

England I never trained every single day, played football every single day, and I was never given the opportunities that people have got now in terms of like physio, nutrition, psychology, all that kind of stuff. I would have liked to sort of soak all that up and see how good I could have been, really.'

Handley thought that some players of her generation and older could well be justified if they looked at the current crop of professionals and wondered if they realised their good fortune, or how hard other women had fought to gain them those opportunities. She wanted to see former players' contributions recognised and praised much more extensively, with people like Gill Coultard acknowledged as a legend.

'They need to be recognising the commitment that these people made,' she said. 'At that time they were the elite. They were the best and they didn't have the opportunities that people have got now.

'Gill Coultard – what an amazing achievement caps-wise, and she gets really no recognition for that. If we weren't to tell people our past, no one would ever know. People like that, who played hundreds of times for England, played in World Cups, people should know who they are. The girls now ought to know that they were the people who paved the way.'

Gill Coultard's football playing days ended at the age of 36, and although she sometimes wondered if she could have carried on for longer, she was content with her achievements.

'Probably from a club point of view I could have gone an extra year,' she admitted, 'but I just thought I'd given 21 years to football and for England especially, and I just thought I couldn't do that [any more]. Now I just think, "How did I find the time to do all the things I did?"'

It had been one of the great puzzles of women's football that she had not been recognised in any honours list when players before and after her had been, and that omission was finally rectified in the 2021 New Year's Honours List when she was appointed a Member of the British Empire, or MBE for short.

Karen Walker looked out for the Belles' results, but admitted that she did not really see the current club as the same one as she had played for.

'Doncaster Belles is a different entity, completely different; they play in completely different colours, everything about it,' she said, adding that Sheila Edmunds was the only constant and the sole link back to the Belles' foundations.

Walker still kicked a ball round occasionally with her male colleagues. They knew of her footballing pedigree, and she got plenty of ribbing for it. 'You'd think it would be a really good thing, but I get more stick,' she said, adding placidly: 'I don't mind it!'

Debbie Biggins, who as a teenager had played alongside Walker and Coultard for Belles, described herself as a former but not yet retired goalkeeper. She continued to turn out for impromptu works matches and charity games when required, but her usual team-mates now were not England internationals but television stars.

That was because Biggins' life had been entirely changed by the BBC documentary on the Belles. Celebrated scriptwriter Kay Mellor had watched it and been inspired to write her series *Playing the Field*, about a women's football team and their lives on and off the pitch. Biggins was one of the players invited to take part in the on-field scenes, and, with a background in coaching, ended up advising the actors and production staff on how to make the fictionalised matches look more realistic. That gave her the bug for television, getting a job shortly afterwards as a runner, then an assistant director, and on to her role as producer of one of the BBC's biggest and most established dramas, *Casualty*.

'At school they told me not to go [to join up with the England squad], not to do that, it was ridiculous and I'd never get anywhere through playing football,' Biggins recalled. 'Actually, I've got exactly where I wanted through playing football!'

Biggins was at the top of her game while still very young, whereas many goalkeepers tend to come into their own when slightly older. She thought that when she was at Belles, she still had a lot to learn, but with so little specialised goal-keeping coaching in the women's game, perhaps some of her skills had been neglected, despite her managers doing their best.

'Goalkeepers – we still are a bit further behind than every-body else, and I think the standard of goalkeepers is slightly lower in women's football,' she said, 'but it's hard to have that mentality. I'm quite happy to get my face kicked! And you're shorter, it's just a physical thing, but goals are the same size – I am only five [foot] seven now – and that is a big area to cover. There wasn't much goalkeeping around or many goalkeeping coaches at all. But I was lucky that being young as soon as I finished school I was at Burnley and I was at Doncaster Rovers [coaching and studying for her National Vocational Qualifications] and we did get to play with the men, so that helped a lot with the physicality side of it – that I was playing with men and I had the speed of the shots from men.'

As a young player, Biggins admired male goalkeepers – Dave Beasant, Chris Woods and Peter Shilton, a trio of England internationals, were her top three role models. 'They were just steady. They weren't like the crazy goalkeepers – they were just steady, good positioning, and that's what I always wanted to do, just be in the right positions at the right times, and then that helps with everything else.'

Biggins was now usually the only woman on a team full of men when she turned out for a TV show's side, a far cry from her time with the all-conquering Belles.

'I don't have a club that I play for, I just sort of play for pleasure, really,' she said, 'and it's nearly always with men. I can't remember the last time that I played with women.'

Belles past and present were brought together for the saddest of reasons in May 2021, mourning the death of Julie Chipchase. Chippy had been a player in the 1980s, progressing to manage the reserve side and then the first team, and although she left for a spell as boss at Leeds United, Belles was her first footballing love. Her honours included three FA Cup wins as a player and two runners-up medals as a manager with Belles. A fine coach – one of the first women to obtain a UEFA A licence, and later a Pro licence – she had been involved with a number of the England junior squads. Alongside her great friend and collaborator Sheila Edmunds, she had sat on the Belles board to shape its strategy after dropping out of the WSL.

Even some months afterwards, Sue Smith, the former England international, could barely believe that a person as vibrant and passionate as Chippy had gone. When she had heard that her coach and friend was gravely ill, she had wanted to visit, but had not been able to.

'Oh, it was just so, so sad,' she said. 'Afterwards we were all saying, "I just wished we'd have contacted her more or got to see her more." She meant so much to us all.'

Smith's first encounter with Chippy was in 2002, as a 21-year-old player for Tranmere Rovers, studying at Edge Hill University in Ormskirk, Lancashire, and looking to progress her England career. She had already made her senior debut as a teenager, but wanted to become a permanent fixture in the side and improve her skills, and to do that, it looked likely that she would need to leave Tranmere for a bigger club. She spoke to three managers – Vic Akers at Arsenal, Mark Hodgson at Leeds, and Chipchase at Doncaster Belles. London was just too far away for a young woman who wanted to stay at home as well as complete her degree course, so it was down to two options.

'I remember taking my mum and dad to Doncaster, and we met Chippy, and I had a training session with her, and then I went to Leeds to do exactly the same thing,' she recalled. 'And I just remember that Leeds was more – I don't want to say professional because that wasn't the case – it was more like they trained at Thorp Arch [the men's club's training ground], they had real backing from the chairman and it seemed like this was the team that could potentially progress and go and challenge Arsenal.

'Chippy was the major pull at Donny, and I remember speaking to Mum and Dad and they would just say, "She's brilliant. She's lovely, she speaks so well." She obviously had a real football brain and she knew what to say, as a player coming to sign for you – but she also just had a nice way about her.

'And that was the thing that was the hardest thing to say no to! Then she kept in contact because we spoke then, there was no agents or anything like that. She just used to ring and say, "You could still come to us any time!"'

Smith had done her research on Chipchase, speaking to England team-mate Karen Walker who enthused about her – and the more she got to know her, the more she wanted to be coached by her. Her decision to sign for Leeds rather than Chipchase's Belles, strangely, was the route to achieving that; in 2003, Chippy took over the United hotseat.

'It's what she does other than the football side, because I think you just take that for granted,' said Smith, lapsing into the present tense without thinking about it. 'She's a top-quality coach, she's an A-licence coach, she's one of the first females to get her A licence so that's just aside – she's very good at that and picking out things in the game and able to change things in a game, but it was more that she cares for you as a person.'

Smith had better reason than most to remember the care Chippy showed for her players. In 2005, the two had been talking about how Smith could improve her all-round game and become an even more important part of the England side. The European Championships were being held in England that summer, and Smith was desperate to shine.

Then she got a phone call from England boss Hope Powell to tell her she had not been selected for the final squad. The next time Smith's phone rang, it was Chippy. Heartbroken, she did not answer, and let it ring through to voicemail. When she picked up the message, she was surprised at its contents.

'She said, "I just want you to know, we're absolutely gutted for you. I know we've got training tonight, you don't need to come, it's entirely up to you, but we're all here for you, whatever you need to do, whether it's talk football, or whether it's talk about something else."

'And I just thought that was so nice. I don't know how many other managers would have done that – I think they would in time, but Chippy was the first person to actually do that and ring up, and I just thought that was lovely. Not that I didn't have respect for her before that, because I did, but just even more so, because she had, I suppose, the courage to do that.

'And I did – I went to training!'

Developing players was one of Chipchase's major delights; that was particularly the case at Belles, where the family ethos continues to run deep. The Belles juniors were not necessarily the best players in the country for their age groups, but they had the chance to work on their talent and become the best players they could become.

'You could see these youngsters coming through that obviously had a little bit of talent, but she just brought that forward, and she must have had so much pride seeing those players develop, seeing those players flourishing, playing in the WSL, some of them going on to play international football,' said Smith. 'You could just imagine her, like she looked after me, doing the same for these young players. And I think you always remember that, don't you? You always remember the first manager that actually took a real interest in you as a person.

'I've had managers that just want to win, they just want to get the best out of the team, but they're not really bothered about what your other life is, if you like. It's not that [it] isn't of interest to them, it's just about the football, and just about focusing on that, whereas Chippy – I suppose you'd call it like a holistic approach now. She's interested in everything about you, not in a nosy way, but what makes you tick.'

That scorn for the prioritisation of winning over everything else was deeply bred in Belles' bones. Then-manager Paul Edmunds had vented his fury at what he saw as the 'profession-alism' of Arsenal when his Belles side had lost to them 3–1 in the 1995 Women's FA Cup final; he detested gamesmanship, and time-wasting, and all the little things you might see in the men's game as a team chased a win and did not care how they achieved it. Chipchase, who played in many of Edmunds' successful Belles teams, shared that philosophy.

'I remember in the FA [Women's] Cup Final [in 2006], we got absolutely tonked by Arsenal [5–0], and I remember just looking over at Chippy and just being so gutted,' said Smith. 'Obviously I was gutted myself and gutted for the team, but I was gutted for her. You just think, "I would have loved to have just won it for you." That was the relationship that we all had with her. You don't often get that. She was certainly one of a kind. I would be saying that if she was still here – it's not just a case of we've lost her and we're all really sad and we're saying really nice things about her. I think if you spoke to any player that was managed by Chippy, they will say exactly the same.'

Alex Culvin had first met Chipchase as a teenager; Chippy was working in the England youth set-up when Culvin was on a camp. She had been impressed by the warmth that emanated from this highly experienced, highly qualified coach. A few years later, when Culvin was not getting regular time in the Everton first team, Chipchase suggested she sign for Doncaster Belles. It was hugely flattering and also daunting for a very young player, but she nevertheless had absolute faith in her coach's judgement.

'We had a really good rapport, me and Chippy,' said Culvin. 'I challenged her a lot. I'd ask questions, like, "Why are we doing it this way?" or whatever. She took it well – sometimes she'd say shut up,' she stopped to laugh, 'but sometimes she'd take me to one side and maybe explain the intricacies of the game. I always considered myself to be a bit of a student of the game. I loved it, I was always keen to learn things. I really valued that one-on-one time with Chippy.'

Culvin knew some of the senior Belles players already at the club, including Jody Handley, who had been at Everton at the same time. Still, she was apprehensive when she arrived there.

'Doncaster Belles were the best team in the league by some stretch, we had the best players, and it was like a kid going into a woman's dressing room – I was really nervous!' she said. 'And Chippy just made me feel at home straight away; she gave me a voice in the dressing room, she gave me responsibility, and she just really had that knack of getting the best out of you as well.'

A year later, when Chipchase made the shock move across Yorkshire to local rivals Leeds, Culvin was one of the Belles players she took with her.

'Leeds had loads of money, they had a really good backing at the time,' explained Culvin. 'She just said, "I'm taking you with me," and I was just like, "Oh, OK then, yeah," and then it became this real big rivalry between [Leeds and Belles], and obviously it's a derby anyway.

'But I always thought Chippy was really brave for doing that because she was at Belles, she played for Belles, she was from Doncaster, Doncaster was her life, and she moved on to better herself at Leeds, for funding, all of that type of stuff, and she wanted to develop players even further. I remember thinking, "Bloody hell, she's brave doing that," because the rivalry was huge then, and, yeah, it was always something I admired in her – it was a real quiet bravery and confidence in what she was doing.'

Chipchase's other major passion was encouraging the talent pipeline for female coaches. She was very well aware of how tough it could be for an aspiring football coach, particularly a woman in a still male-dominated field, and like Belles as a club, Chippy was committed to giving women the opportunity to coach and to lead. Just in the few years prior to her death, Belles provided incredible career breaks for Emma Coates and Zoey Shaw, both relative novices when given the first-team job. Coates left to work with the England youth set-up, Shaw continued her pursuit of an A licence.

'She was really an advocate of pushing women,' agreed Culvin, 'and I think Belles fitted that perfectly at the time, because we were an independent club, and we were a successful club. It wasn't like she was going round saying, "I'm a feminist and I'm doing this for feminism," and all of these types of stuff – it was just her general model and belief that women should be given opportunities because they're not. Her team talks would be very focused on us about what we can do as a group of women.

'I probably just took that for granted when I played because that's just how Chippy operated; it was unique and it is unique still now.'

One of the many coaches Chipchase mentored was Sally Needham, part of the FA's coach education scheme, who became part of the Belles coaching set-up – and went on to become an A-licence holder herself.

'I can remember it plain as day,' she recalled, thinking back to a conversation in 2015, when she was working at Sheffield United's regional talent centre. 'I was at a works do – we used to have these away days at the FA, at St George's Park – and she said to me, "I want you in my office," and it was just a table. She said, "Do you fancy coming and doing the development team at Belles?"'

Although Needham had spoken to Chipchase before, she did not know her well – only by reputation. Over the next few years, they worked together at Belles and also at the FA, and became close friends as Needham began to assume some of Chipchase's workload to encourage more female coaches at Belles. Although they had a male goalkeeping coach for the first team, the majority of the rest of the set-up was staffed by women.

'She wanted to develop the females and give them an opportunity,' said Needham, 'but also she looked for people that had certain characters in them, certain traits that she really wanted as people.

'She were very brave and put Emma [Coates] in – [she was] only 25 when she went in at WSL [as head coach]. I think with Chippy she saw what human qualities somebody had . . . if they could be coming to her philosophy and they fitted our philosophy, she brought them in. She realised that a lot of the females have got the mindset and the capability to go on. She challenged you, she wanted you to change as well as affect society a little bit.

'She gave them the skill set and the confidence and little words of wisdom, to let them then go and then fly. There's nobody really done a sideward step, everybody's moved up and forward with their career.'

As one of her closest friends, Needham spent time with Chipchase in the days before her death, and made her a promise. 'Chippy asked me when she wasn't very well [in] the last week before she passed away, she said, "Don't let people forget me." I said that I wouldn't. Her legacy will be carrying on anyway because she's influenced so many people that's in the game.'

The two spoke most days, and Needham appreciated Chipchase's exhortations for courage and risk-taking as well as her calm assessment of problems; she would not tell people what they should do, but encourage reflection and consideration.

'She was one of my best friends,' said Needham, holding back tears. 'She mentored me on the pitch, but then I spoke to her every single day, more or less, on my way home from work, about work and about life. So, yeah, I miss her terribly.'

'The passing of Chippy was really, really heartbreaking,' said Culvin. 'She was just an incredible person, she was funny, she was caring and she was a great coach. I think the women's game is moving rapidly towards mirroring the men's game in lots of ways that we probably don't really want, that's the way things are happening, and I think Chippy did things differently. She put humans first before winning games, she put an arm round the players if they needed it.

'I'd like to remember Chippy standing with a little half of lager – she never had a pint, always a half – she was just amazing. We remember her first and foremost as a friend, coach, someone we loved very much, mum to Charlie and Lily and partner to Jo.'

TEN

THE CHAMPIONS

VIC AKERS WAS THE MAN tasked with establishing a women's set-up at the mighty Arsenal. A left-back in his own playing days, he had a wide-ranging remit at Highbury, taken on by Don Howe to do some scouting for the first team, but also to head up the club's community department. The Greater London Council wanted more officers in professional football clubs working to bring in local people and to connect them with their community. This came in the middle of the 1980s, when incidences of football hooliganism garnered much media attention and much horror in the halls of power.

Akers set up sporting activities for people of all ages, and it was one of his community team who gave him the idea to get involved in women's football. 'The girl that I employed was actually a female footballer from the Aylesbury area,' he recalled. 'We began to talk and I got interested in the women's game through her, and suggested maybe that we try and form a club itself, and I would go to the board and see if we could create off our own back and see how it went. And that was how it happened.'

Akers spoke to director David Dein, who argued the case to the rest of the board, including a very supportive Ken Friar, the club's managing director.

'It was good days then,' said Akers. 'There were a couple of young girls that played in local football around Islington, and they came to the sessions, the early girls' sessions, and said, "We would love to be part of the new team," and one of them actually went on to play for England, Michelle Curley, left-back for England, so that was good. And it just developed really from there.'

Gill Sayell, who had been part of the unofficial national team in Mexico, was a founder member of Akers' new Arsenal squad in 1987. She lived and worked in Aylesbury, and her father had set up a club in the town in 1976 after a rift in the squad meant her previous club Thame folded. He had also joined the board of directors at the men's club Aylesbury United, which meant that the women's team were able to use their pitch and facilities on a Sunday afternoon – after the men had played there on a Saturday and churned it up.

When Aylesbury United sold their ground, the women started playing in Cuddington, a nearby village. By July 1987, they had become Arsenal Ladies, playing a friendly in Milton Keynes, with Sayell, just back from giving birth to her daughter, as part of the squad.

Akers concurred with that memory. 'They were getting to their later years, as it were, all together, and we took their place in the league and put it in as Arsenal, and that was where it all formed from.'

'Vic changed my game,' said Sayell. 'I used to be an outside right-winger, and he put me at centre-back – bearing in mind I'm really just over five foot tall. But I so enjoyed it – I can read a game, and he put me back there and I played my best football there. The coaching, it was second to none, from what we'd had. Playing for Aylesbury, Thame and the like, it was people volunteering to go out there and train us and coach us and everything. But with a more professional set-up, you did feel different, for sure.'

Sayell would travel to Highbury for training twice a week with the rest of the squad, with their sessions on a carpeted pitch underneath the Clock End, open to the elements. Later, they had access to the indoor facilities in the JVC Centre, training from around 9 p.m. until 11 p.m.

'We'd get changed in the ground, in the changing rooms,' she said. 'We'd come out and we'd run around the streets of Highbury. We'd do all that and then we used to do drills around the pitch, up and down the terraces.

'They had a small gym as well, at the front of Highbury, above the changing rooms at the top. We used to go in there as well and train in there. It was a leap up from what we had had, but thinking back now, it was still quite basic.'

Akers also tried to bring in plenty of established top talent.

'He mithered the living daylights out of me!' laughed Liz Deighan. She opted to stay with St Helens rather than move to London, mostly because she wanted to stay in her day job. 'They were really good to me. They never made me take holidays when I went away with England.

'Vic is and was a great guy, I really enjoy talking to him. But there was no guarantee of employment [if] I went down there. It was all, "Oh, well, we'll get you a job within the community [department]." But I think I was nervous about leaving a good job to do something I was pretty uncertain about.'

'When we first started, in the early years . . . we tried to run three teams, because we had so many players who wanted to come to the club and join,' said Akers. 'We were able to bring in players from Millwall, who at the time were the best team in London by a mile, and then people like Brenda Sempare, Hope Powell, Sian Williams who actually came to me as well to play and was a captain in one of my teams. So all of a sudden times were changing in women's football.

'And people could see that – [men's] clubs coming in, senior clubs and taking on sides, was the way forward. We tried to make sure that other people knew how we worked, and we shared that with people as well, such as Liverpool and Everton and people like that. We shared the way that we organised, the way we did it. And people would come up to us to ask advice for that, which I thought was really nice, that they respected us that much that they could work with us in that respect. Of course I was more than willing to offer any advice that we could.'

Sayell still had her teamsheets from the first days of Arsenal Ladies. 'It was a great era,' she said. 'The girls were there together and wanting to do the same thing – just play football.'

She had considered giving up football after having her daughter. Her parents had moved to Menorca, and she and her husband were intending to move their family over there too. The lure of football, however, proved too strong.

'We were halfway through the season – three months left of the season,' she explained. 'So my husband and my daughter went with my mum and dad, and I stayed here to play the rest of the season. I didn't want to miss it.'

She joined them in the summer, but couldn't settle, and once again returned to England, rejoining the Arsenal squad.

'My parents said, "Well, you know, if that's what you need to do,"' she recalled, adding that her husband had not been best pleased.

Sayell played on until 1993, when she was 36, and could no longer maintain her high performance levels after knee injuries. 'I think I maybe got [the injuries] playing in the ball court. In the astroturf, your foot stays still, and your knee twists, and I had had a couple of cartilage operations on that same knee previous, so it's probably going to be a bit weak anyway. But I would have carried on if I could, even at that age.'

Faye White had a very striking memory of the day she signed for Arsenal.

'That was in 1996,' she said. 'I always remember the year because it was the year [Arsene] Wenger joined [as manager of the men's team], so I remember.

'My first impression of it was pretty much driving to London, to the Highbury stadium, to meet Vic – he'd come down to see me and my family to talk about the club before that – driving under to the car park . . . and then he took us through some corridors and I thought, "Ah, we're just going down to his office or something."

'But he opened this door and it was one of the boxes which looked over the Clock End of Highbury, and he was like, "Just walk in here."

'I was just like, "Oh, my God."'

White had just turned 18, and although the contract was signed without broadcasters or photographers to record the moment, the introduction to Highbury and to Arsenal was a special one.

Before signing for Arsenal, White had played her football on parks in Sussex, joining Horsham, later Three Bridges, as a child. She was at sixth-form college, and had been considering going to Loughborough University but was worried that the England coaches would not keep tabs on her progress if she was not playing club football regularly. Instead, she became a fitness instructor at a local health club when she finished her A-levels. She knew about the Gunners' history as a women's side; they were on the rise and had already won a number of trophies before she was approached by them. Her ability had also caught the eye of another leading club at the time – Croydon.

'Croydon asked me to join them too, at the time, but their manager went away on holiday for two weeks and said, "I'll talk to you when I get back," and Vic had been down in the meantime to see me,' said White. She had impressed him in the previous season when Three Bridges had played Arsenal in the Women's FA Cup, and the 17-year-old had been given the tough task of marking England international Marieanne Spacey.

'I had the best game of my life,' said White. 'I was just like, "Right, I'm ready for this." That was my mentality: I wanted to play and be against the best. But I was so nervous!'

Even though she was not playing at the top level of the domestic game, White had already been called up to England training camps, so Akers asked one of her international team-mates to speak to her about whether she might be interested in a move to Arsenal. White and the Three Bridges coach had already had a conversation about whether she would need to move on if she had hopes of a long international career, so she was prepared for the prospect. She got Akers' phone number and gave him a call, and he said he would travel to Sussex to meet her.

That first formal meeting with Akers was a rather unusual one. 'We met in McDonald's just outside the South terminal at Gatwick, because that's the only place I could think of!' she laughed. 'He said, "What do you want?" and I said, "A cup of tea" – I'm not going to order food, am I, that's not the best image to give him! So we had a cup of tea in McDonald's.'

Akers also dropped in to meet White's family. They were understandably slightly apprehensive about their teenage daughter travelling all the way to North London for training and then coming home again; at that point, it meant a train journey from Gatwick Airport to King's Cross and then on the Piccadilly Line to Arsenal tube station, next to Highbury Stadium. To take away some of the nerves for the first few weeks, Akers would pick White up from King's Cross to save her having to take the underground, as he did for some of the other players who had lengthy journeys or were new to the city.

'I remember the first season I played for Arsenal, I would just go home after every game and I'd have a little league table on my computer,' said White. 'I'd be marking who scored what. I just wouldn't want to switch off from it, when I was young.'

White carried on making that journey for the best part of a decade. At first it was once a week, but it became two days out of seven. She would work 6 a.m. until 2 p.m. at the health club, making the two-hour journey into London, training from 8 p.m. until 10 p.m., getting home at midnight and then getting up the next morning for work as usual. In 2005, when Arsenal Women were sharing the men's training facility in London Colney, White was working for the club, and moved up to the area to share a house with striker Kelly Smith; it coincided with England hosting the Women's European Championships, by which time she was the national skipper.

'At that time, when we moved our offices up to the training ground, I was driving around the M25 every day,' she said. 'I was working for the club at that time as well as the development officer, so I drove around two hours, sometimes three hours there, because it's the M25, and I thought, "I can't do this as well as train and publicise the 2005 Euros."

'We just shared a bungalow in London Colney. It wasn't very glamorous but it allowed me to be close and dedicate more time to rest and recovery as opposed to driving.'

As a little girl growing up in Ireland, Yvonne Tracy always supported Arsenal. When she began playing football for her country, she knew managers in England would be watching her, but there was only ever one team she wanted to sign for, and the opportunity arrived in the summer of 2000, when she travelled for a week's trial with the Gunners, along with compatriots Caroline Thorpe and Susan Heapes.

'I had my mind made up before I came over, if I'm being honest,' she said. There were already plenty of Irish players in the squad, including her international team-mates Emma Byrne and Ciara Grant, so she felt comfortable as soon as she arrived. 'There were so many of us, you couldn't even get homesick. There were about seven or eight of us at the time. It was a case of home from home.'

Tracy and her team-mates moved into a flatshare at the entrance to the West Stand at Arsenal's then-home ground, Highbury, and she began a job at the club's box office along with Byrne before moving to a role at the training ground. When she left Dublin she had also left behind an unfinished college course; the demands of international football had meant that she could not attend classes as regularly as was required, and it became apparent that she would not be able to complete the qualification.

'I couldn't catch up with what I was doing,' she said. 'I just packed it in. I just got a job in the local shop at home and then moved straight from there.'

The facilities Arsenal gave their women to train on were beyond the dreams of most female footballers at the time. They had access to some of the same pitches and equipment as the men did, even if they had to wait for the male players to finish before they could start their session, which often meant very long days.

It also meant some creative thinking for fitness training if there was no availability in the gym.

'We used to train Tuesdays and Thursdays at Highbury, and the first hour was just running,' said Tracy. 'It was either running around the track, or it was up and down the steps [on the terraces], just a solid hour of running, non-stop, and then we'd go in and play in the ball court area at the JVC Centre [the indoor club facility] for another hour . . . the intensity was so good because you could play off the wall so it was a case of one hour of solid . . .' Tracy paused to think of the right noun, and she could not think of an appropriate one to describe the competitiveness and the passion in a straightforward training session. '. . . Just battered.'

'I couldn't!' laughed White about her first-ever Arsenal training session and the prospect of all that running. 'I was overawed, too nervous, and I kept going dizzy. So I sat that out but joined in the football bit a bit later.'

'They worked very hard, going into the stands and running up and down stairs, which the club allowed us to do,' said Vic Akers. 'That was excellent, because it did, in effect, do what I really wanted to do, which was to make the girls more athletic rather than in all shapes and sizes at the time which we all were. I pointed out to them privately, "Listen, you know, if we want to be taken seriously we have to make a better use of our fitness, make sure that we are more athletic-looking than what we are at the moment. We need to get those levels of fitness up to a higher standard."'

Akers tried to instil as much professionalism as he could, and his dedication to the cause meant that he had very little free time to himself bearing in mind his work across both sides of the club. He described his working hours as 'eight days a week . . . always devoted to the club and to women's football as well as men's football', travelling on a Saturday to watch a men's game, then coaching the women on a Sunday.

He loved every moment.

'I could see what was unfolding in front of me, providing we took it in the right way – it would be fabulous for the sport,' he said, recalling a match where he went into the clubhouse after an away match and saw some of his players enjoying a drink at the bar. 'I said to the girls on the bus home, "We'll have a meeting on Tuesday before training so if you can get there 15, 20 minutes early I'd appreciate it because we want to sort one or two things out" – we'd won so I didn't want to kill the spirit at that point because we had three and a half hours to get down the motorway!'

On that Tuesday evening he told his players they needed to think about their behaviour, particularly in front of fans. He admitted that his own teetotalism didn't help their cause, but even if he did drink, he would still say that drinking alcohol at a bar in public after a match wasn't appropriate.

'I said, "Drink something separate like I do, non-alcoholic. When you get home, if that's what you want to do in your private life, that's fine. I'm quite happy with that. Obviously, you'll be the losers – I won't – because there'll be a time where I can leave you out of the team because your fitness levels are not going to stay with the ones that we're trying to achieve."'

'I feel that they benefited from it in the short term, and I think probably in the long term they benefited from it as well because we only went on to be successful, and hopefully the club was recognised and well respected in the women's game. That was how the main club was, and that's how the women's club should be, all part of the same, and so that's what we tried to achieve.'

Akers' work on improving his squad's fitness helped Arsenal's style of play on the pitch that took them to the very pinnacle of the game. Even the limitations of the indoor facilities – bouncing the ball off the walls and back into play – helped, because the players became used to quick, one-touch passing, having to improve their speed of thought and decision-making. Because the club had the resources to offer players jobs, they were also immersed in the world of football, and never had problems making training or a game because of work commitments, and the women made good use of the London Colney complex once it opened its doors to them. Eventually, players like White also had contracts with England, meaning that they increased their training, able to work in the gym by themselves even if they were not able to train together as a squad.

'We would have training sessions in the morning at, like, six o'clock,' said White. 'Some days three or four of us would do a little session, or sometimes on our own, like out on the field, with a coach that the FA had paid for, to train with, or we would do a gym session or something. Then I would go into the office say, half nine, ten sometimes depending on when I'd got changed and stuff, and then sometimes go into schools doing coaching or assemblies, and work till three, four-ish.

'And then we'd train normally – when we first started training at the training ground it was still in the evening, so it was like a six or seven o'clock kind of time. I was one of the fortunate ones because I had a job that I loved doing for the club.

'But when I first joined . . . I remember a couple of years ago when we were clearing out the [club] office I found a little book that Vic had kept the subs in – a list of all the names of who'd paid a fiver or a tenner for match fees. Oh, my God! Some of the names in there – like Gill Wylie [later the Charlton player-manager], lots of older players. I paid when I first joined, not glamorous, but you still paid your subs. So I know that time it was still, like, "Wow, I'm playing for Arsenal!"'

Anita Asante was snapped up by Arsenal as a teenager. She lived in North London, and her school was notified of a centre of excellence session the club was hosting in the area. She went along, the coaches – who included players Rachel Yankey and Clare Wheatley – were impressed with her, and she was invited to go along to regular training sessions.

There was just one problem. The regular junior training was held in Hackney, involving a lengthy and convoluted journey via public transport for the 14-year-old Asante, who would have had to head almost straight out to East London after finishing school to make an 8 p.m. session. Fortunately, her father was supportive, and not only that, but he worked nights, meaning he was around to drive her from Edgware to Hackney twice a week. He dropped her off, waited for her, and then took her home again – still a trek, but not as time-consuming as travelling by train and underground.

As a youngster, Asante was playing up front, and once she was part of the Arsenal junior teams, who trained out in High Barnet, Vic Akers got word of a teenage striker who was worth a look. Asante remembered the words from her coach giving her the heads-up that the first-team manager would be watching that evening.

'"Vic's going to be in the session today, he's heard lots about you, he wants to see you, playing as a forward, as a striker,"' recalled Asante. 'I knew it was a big deal. This is the head of the women's team – that's the first time that I saw him and I felt his presence and I wanted to impress. He didn't say many words, he wasn't a man of many words then, probably still isn't today. I just remember that whole experience – and honestly I knew that I didn't have the ego to be a forward, for sure! I was always passing the ball, and my coach was like, "You need to not pass the ball, like, go for it," and things like that, but, yeah, I think [Vic was] still intrigued, interested, or impressed with what he saw, and it went from there.'

Asante was called up to join the senior squad, and her first vivid memories of stepping up was the intensity of the training sessions at Highbury. 'I remember the indoor sessions in the evenings with the likes of Sian Williams and Casey Stoney and all those guys,' she said, 'and there'd be a few of us, two or three of us from my age group would join, and we'd have a couple of sessions and I just think from then on that's when Vic took notice and then would include me in in the senior team.'

'The training was actually more competitive than the games we played, certainly when I was over for the first couple of years,' said Tracy. 'The standard [in the league] wasn't great. We were winning like eight, nine most weekends.'

As a defender, Tracy found herself getting a little bored – although she found herself properly tested when she represented Ireland.

'I knew both sides of the story,' she said. 'I wasn't used to just winning all the time, I knew how it was to lose, so I think that made me more humble or gracious in defeat as well as winning, because I know it's not nice to lose by many goals.

'But it was tough to keep it going, especially if you're not going up for corners or getting involved in the game, because you're literally just stood at the back doing nothing. It was a case of, "Can I go up now for a corner or a free kick?" or something like that.'

As a relatively novice defender, Asante found herself learning a lot from the senior players very quickly.

'If we were at 100 per cent, if we were at 70 per cent, there was never a doubt in my mind that we wouldn't win,' she said, 'mostly because we had drivers in the team, if that makes sense. You have people like Kelly [Smith] obviously that can make things happen, individually, but you also have leaders like Jayne Ludlow. She was never afraid to tell you what's what, and just be real on the pitch. She could shout and scream and all of that, but sometimes we needed that, we needed that kick, that push, that reminder of our own standards, individually and collectively. Any time it would happen I always felt like, "Yes, this is because she knows we're better than this, she knows we can do more," and you need people like that [on] your team. Playing alongside Ciara [Grant] as well . . . her experience – she wasn't a very commanding person vocally, but the sense of trust I had playing alongside her was unquestionable. I just knew she'd be in the right position, I knew she would communicate with me, I trusted in her ability on the ball – that sense of security.'

*

'The biggest highlight was 2007, when we won all four trophies including the European [the UEFA Women's Cup, the equivalent of today's Champions League],' said Vic Akers, looking back on his decades with the club. 'That has not been accomplished by any other club, and with respect, because standards have changed so much, I don't think it will be.'

Prior to Arsenal's run in the competition, no team outside Germany or the Scandinavian countries – the traditional strongholds of women's football in Europe – had ever reached the UEFA Women's Cup final. The ties were all played over two legs, necessitating a great deal of travel across the continent. In the quarter-final, they got a 9–1 aggregate win over Breidablik from Iceland, but in the semi-final, they had a much tougher task against Brøndby of Denmark. In the away leg, Kelly Smith put her side ahead twice but the hosts equalised twice. Smith was sent off late on after losing her temper and retaliating to a string of fouls she had suffered, meaning she was going to miss the next three matches of European competition – that is, she would not be available for the home leg plus both legs of the final should Arsenal progress. Goals from Rachel Yankey, Karen Carney and Julie Fleeting secured a win against the Danish side back at Meadow Park to put the Smith-less Arsenal into the final against Sweden's Umeå.

There was only one goal across either leg, and it came from an unexpected source – right-back Alex Scott, who struck a spectacular effort in the first match in Sweden. It may have been slightly wind-assisted, but it was certainly deliberate; in the final seconds of the game, literally in added time, Scott was making a run up the right wing, and her manager, very conscious of the seconds ticking away, urged her to shoot. She put her head down and did as she was told, and was perhaps the most surprised person in the ground when she saw it hit the back of the net.

In the second leg, Arsenal's courageous defending nullified the attacking threat of Umea's superstar Brazilian striker Marta, and they lifted the trophy on their home turf in Borehamwood. The fact that Arsenal were depleted of their talismanic Kelly Smith in that final was overlooked by many observers, thought Akers.

'We had arguably the best player in the world not playing – and the other team had Marta,' he said. 'It was a bigger success than most people think.'

'I remember today Alex's goal,' said Asante. 'I remember the pressure of this onslaught from this very good side that was attacking us all the time, and me and Ciara were having to be like super alert and extremely concentrated. I remember feeling all of that, the tension and stuff, and then obviously the home leg, I think there was a sense of "Yes, we got the win away, and we knew it wasn't an easy task, we got it done", and then at home it was, "We're halfway there – everybody, we die for the cause. Do whatever you can, in any situation. We know they're a good team, we know they'll probably get some opportunities."

'And I remember all of us saying afterwards – the minute Marta hit the ball, and it hit the post or the crossbar and then it bounced off Emma Byrne's head or something and it went out . . . we were just like, "This is our day, 100 per cent, this is our day, there is no way in normal circumstances that is not a goal, or that is not going in."'

Akers concurred that was the moment he knew his team would win the cup. 'I thought, "Oh, my God," and it went wide of the same post it had hit,' he said. 'Thankfully, Emma's head was that shape! And I thought, "That's it, we're going to win this."'

'That was the best season,' said Tracy. 'Player-wise, it was insane: like, Kelly Smith, Alex Scott, Emma Byrne, Jayne Ludlow, Julie Fleeting, the works – the captains of nearly every country, Wales, Scotland and England, the talent was just ridiculous, like even on the bench, and everything was just quality the whole way through.'

'Everybody worked so hard,' added Akers. 'Jayne Ludlow must have covered every inch of grass on Boreham Wood's pitch [in the second leg], she was just perpetual motion all over the place, never stopped. I had to bring her off at the end because she'd got a booking – I thought if she goes in and makes another tackle we're going to go down to ten men and then we're in trouble. I just had to bring her off because she would never have forgiven herself [if she had been sent off].

'Everybody just worked so hard to achieve what we thought we could do – coming back from Sweden 1–0 ahead with and Alex Scott scoring the goal from 25, 30 yards in the last moments of the game out there was a phenomenal result for us, which we weren't going to give up lightly. We never did.'

'I think to do what we did then with what we didn't have is a huge thing – we weren't professionals as such, we were training twice a week,' pointed out Asante. 'But the spirit of the team and the players and the belief is something you can't always find. It's testament to the characters we had. We were playing teams in Europe that we knew were much more consolidated in the sense of training and things like that – the Scandinavian teams or German teams. But everyone saw this bigger goal that we could get to and fortunately for us, we did.'

Tracy had missed much of the season, although she was on the bench as an unused substitute for both legs of the UEFA Women's Cup final. She was just recovering from a cruciate ligament injury.

'It was in a game,' she said, 'so I was shielding the ball, it was going out of play, at Bristol Rovers, I think it was at the time. I was blocking the ball and she just came through the side of me. It [the ligament] was still hanging on, so they didn't want to operate but I was still out for six months even though I didn't get surgery.

'And then we were playing Everton, and I was running back towards my own goal, and I just looked over my shoulder behind to see where the girl [opponent] was, and as I turned, as my head turned, it [the knee] just went from underneath me. Disaster.'

Tracy went home for the first two months of her recovery because she was unable to work or even stand. Her mother and sister travelled to London to bring her home via the boat because she was not permitted to fly with her injury. After that, she returned to England, and although she still could not work, the club were supportive, and helped where they could with her rehab.

'Yeah, it was grim, I'm not going to lie,' she said. 'You're getting treatment every Tuesday and Thursday for maybe an hour if you're lucky, and then you have to go to crack on yourself for the rest of the week. I mean, nowadays there are people out there every single minute of the day with them, be it gym, be it field work, everything – I was getting a programme and literally told to go and do it myself. The lucky thing for me was that I worked at the training ground so if I did ever need any help with anything at all, the physios would always help me out and stuff like that so I was lucky, but it was tough.'

Tracy's footballing career began to wind down slowly after that, with her knee causing her a lot of pain. It became increasingly evident that the new management at Arsenal were building for the future, and the Ireland set-up did not want any players who were not first choices for their club sides. Tracy felt she was putting herself through agonies and psychological stress for no reward.

'I was playing with the Irish team, and I had a meeting with the manager [Sue Ronan], and she said, "You're not really playing much, is there a possibility you could move to another club?"' she recalled, adding that she had to reject the option outright because she needed to stay at Arsenal in order to keep her job at the club and be able to afford to live in London. She told Ronan that the standard in her club training games was better than she might get playing in a league competition, or indeed what players in Ireland were getting every week, and she could get a regular 90 minutes playing for the Arsenal reserves if it was simply match time that was the concern.

'But she said it wasn't enough.

'I was sure that my standard in training, what I was doing week in, week out, training four days a week – it was enough for me, I thought, to play [for Ireland], but she seemed to think not. So it was just a case of, "Do you know what? I think now it's time to call it a day."

'We were training in the ball court at the club and it's on astroturf, and we were training for longer, nearly two hours at a time, and I would literally be crying with the pain in my knee because the training was so intense, but I wasn't getting a break. If you were training Tuesday and Thursday, you had the Wednesday to recover, but we were training Tuesday, Wednesday, Thursday, and my body just wasn't able any more, so I just thought, "That's me done, I'm finished."'

Of course, with her work at the club, Tracy was still in a football environment, so she didn't find herself missing the game too much. 'I do printing shirts, do the washing, then I get the kit ready for the following day, do their boots when they come in from training, make sure everything's ready for training before they go for training, it's a hands-on kind of role.'

Coaching was never an option that appealed to her, but more than two decades after she left her college course in Dublin and packed up everything there to join Arsenal, more recently she started to think about what she might do with the rest of her life. She gained qualifications in personal training via online courses, and secured a scholarship to study strength and conditioning, and considered that there could be a life outside football for her.

'Time is pushing on,' she said. 'I don't have a family of my own, I don't have roots at the minute. I've got it all under my belt for when I do decide I've had enough of football and I'm done with it all.'

Anita Asante had studied for a degree in politics and English while playing, and also took up an administrative job at Arsenal. She had begun a PhD, but opted to leave it aside and concentrate on football, moving on to Chelsea before spells in the USA, Sweden, returning to the blue side of London and then signing for Aston Villa at the age of 35. She was not sure whether she might return to university and complete her thesis, explaining: 'I don't know if I have the will any more, to be honest, to read a billion books a day – my concentration span [has become] worse over the years.'

She had decided to move to a smaller professional club for the last years of her career, wanting to finish on a high after suffering repeated serious injuries, including an anterior cruciate ligament problem while on England duty at the SheBelieves Cup in 2019.

'I didn't want to end my career on an injury,' she said. 'I just wanted to be in a training environment, to enjoy it and try to lend my experience to the younger generation, and I think being at a club like Aston Villa allows me to do that, when they're trying to build a project that we know will take more time. They're not the finished article and they want to expose more players to this level, expose them to what professionalism is, what full-time training is and for a lot of players that's an adjustment.

'But it's a transition, and for some, it'll be more challenging than others. For myself, having been through some of that, like playing in America, training and all that stuff, hopefully I can help some of those players quicker with that transition, and also, living with the kind of pressure you might feel now, especially as the game is getting more competitive and more eyes on everyone in that respect.'

She sometimes thought about what that Arsenal side could have achieved had they been full-time professionals, or even simply had access to the kind of resources that some of the other clubs in Europe boasted.

'All of us, every player, or every individual, tries to make the most of their circumstances,' she said, 'as long as they are determined, they have the will, they work hard, they want to compete – and I think that was there for all of us, because of the spirit of the club as well. We felt part of an Arsenal club that was largely successful both on the men's and the women's side, and so you're already walking into somewhat of a legacy that you want to maintain.

'I have no doubt in my mind that if we had the kind of support and resources infrastructure that's in place today, the levels we could have achieved could have been insane. Obviously it's about the talent but it's about the mentality. It's about the bonds and the networks within a team that makes things happen, the belief, the trust. We had all of that in abundance, without the rest of it [the infrastructure]. So I feel like if we'd had the rest of it, who knows what we as a team or as individuals could have achieved?'

She also had some lingering regrets for some of her teammates, who never got the opportunity to play at a major tournament because their nations never qualified during their playing days, in part because of their home country's lack of investment in the women's game.

'We had a lot of Celts in my team at the time – lots of banter, lots of laughter, all of that,' she said. 'But some of them never got to play on the world stage, for example, for their national teams at major competitions, but who knows what might have been if they had had all of that? [They could have been] even more influential for their national teams. It's all of these what-ifs that we can all look back on.'

Faye White was at Arsenal from their amateur days, through their time of semi-professionalism, right up to turning fully pro. She saw exactly how the club changed.

'I remember signing the first little contract that basically said you would get something like £50 or £100 per game,' she said. 'You're doing that, it's four games a [month], the average wasn't bad. If you came on as a sub, you would get a little bit less, or if you won like the FA Cup or something you'd get like an extra hundred pounds or something.

'When you look back at the money as well as my salary for the job, as well as the playing wage, as well as an England contract when that came in, you think, "I'm living the high life compared to a number of players." That was quite a big change because it suddenly felt like we're getting somewhere. We're getting a bit of reward for the hard work that we're putting in, but equally, if you'd have asked the players at that time, would they have done it without that, they would have gone, "Yeah," because we loved it.'

When White was first called up for England, the squad met at a budget chain hotel in Maidenhead. 'It was just a normal business hotel, basically,' she said with amusement. 'So you'd go in and have your breakfast – they'd cordon a bit off for us, but it was quite open where you would have it, the normal buffet area. So a lot of people were having meetings, or busi-nessmen would sit next to you [in the breakfast room], and you'd go off training, get off the bus and come back, and then you'd go and sit in the spa and you'd be sharing the facilities with everyone!

'Eventually I think we moved to Burnham Beeches because that was the hotel the men were using, so I'm sure that was like around the Euros. Yes, other people used it, but it was a lot more secluded, and we also would have a dining room, which was our own private room.

'We'd always train at Bisham Abbey initially, which was a great facility from the start, to be fair, but you were, literally three or four days before a game, meeting up to go through stuff, like they obviously still do now, but you didn't have as many games [then] and you didn't meet as often.'

White also captained England throughout this time of change, leading them not just in the 2005 Euros, but in the 2009 edition, as well as in the 2007 and 2011 Women's World Cups. She found herself doing more and more media interviews, and garnering more and more attention, although it was not always thoughtful or particularly welcome.

'I think the view with England was that we have to improve this – we have to be out there, tell our message, because if we don't, if we're not proud of it . . .' She paused, and picked up the thread again. 'I got the sense – certainly with England and when I was made captain I got put in front of cameras – a lot of people didn't really want to do that, because people didn't want to talk about women's football, because "it's a bit butch".' The quote marks were tangible. 'But I was like, "Unless we do it and we show that we're not, we're not going to change that."'

Of course, that meant that sometimes matters went to the other extreme, with people desperate to prove that female footballers were ordinary women. One of the FA's marketing brochures from around 2003 used the title 'The Beautiful Game' to promote women's football, and featured several high-profile players in fashion-styled photo shoots. They included goalkeeper Rachel Brown (now Brown-Finnis) in a black evening gown plus jewellery along with her goalkeeping gloves, and a then-21-year-old Katie Chapman, a combative midfielder, in a short skirt, vest top and knee-high boots. It also had a photo of White, in an asymmetrical navy velvet frock and red high heels, with a ball tucked under her arm. The opposite page, which had a short question-and-answer segment with her, featured two smaller photos of her on England duty, and the headline read simply: 'Feminine'. One of the questions she was asked was 'How do guys react to you playing football?'; Chapman was asked the same. The concern to show these top international players as women first and foremost is clear.

'It changed gradually, you know, along the way, but just not quick enough for everyone,' said White of the media coverage women's football received. 'But equally, you've got so much more history to catch up on, I suppose because at that time you'd always be compared to the men. How can you even compare me with [Thierry] Henry or whatever, because they train full-time and get everything done for them. It was just a stupid question that you would get asked. You just keep trying to bat back.'

That wasn't to say that White was a particularly vocal type of person. She was one of the quieter ones in the dressing room, although she was never afraid of shouting on the pitch. She never had a particular ambition to captain either Arsenal or England, but she knew that someone needed to take on the leadership role – step into the spotlight and not be embarrassed by the sport or her achievements.

'I was quite happy to be one that would sit in the background if needed, to do my job,' she said. 'But when [the captaincies came], I rose to it in a way. That brought more out of me, I think. But yeah, when I first did interviews, I was nervous. I was scared. I was a bit like, "Oh, my God, am I going to say something wrong?" All those negative thoughts that a lot of people have, or worries, I had them but I thought, "Oh, come on, I've got to do this." If we want it to be better, you've got to change, you've got to be prepared to do this.

'I could see the other players in the squad or team thinking they wanted it but they didn't want to show how much they loved playing football at the time – typical British way. But you see the Americans, they have confidence, and we need to have that attitude as players. We need to show that and show how much I'm going to dedicate, like get to training early, and I'm not going to care if the other girls are laughing and saying "coach's pet".

'I do still say now playing for your country is amazing, but the next best thing is being that role model. So that's what kind of drove me, I suppose, to do that because I thought, "Well, I never had one." I knew about [Arsenal legend] Marieanne Spacey and obviously Gill Coultard and Hope [Powell] and that, when I joined the England team, but before that when I loved playing football in the garden it was all males. If I was looking up to any females it was Steffi Graf, the tennis player, or Denise Lewis, the heptathlete, so those were my role models. I thought, "I can be that role model – or we can – for these girls."

Vic Akers stepped back from Arsenal Women in 2009. He had been in charge of the team for 22 years. As well as the UEFA Women's Cup, he led his team to eleven FA Women's National Premier Division titles, nine Women's FA Cups, ten League Cups, and five Community Shields. All in all, and bearing in mind the occasionally wobbly record-keeping of the 1980s and 1990s, he is considered to have managed his team to anything between 32 and 36 senior competition wins.

'I might not be the best manager in the world but at the end of the day, I possibly am the most successful,' he reflected. 'That is not about me, it's about the players, the playing staff I had around me – the choice of bringing people in.

'That was one thing that Arsene [Wenger, Arsenal men's long-serving manager] always said to me – "The thing I admire the most," he said, "is the fact that you were able to change teams around without disruption, bring in the other players to make those teams as successful as the previous team. That's a skill that doesn't come to many."'

ELEVEN

THE LOST

AFTER AROUND 20 YEARS OF affiliation and collaboration, the Women's FA handed over control of women's football to the FA in 1993. Although they had been running the women's competitions and the England team for decades, with their reliance on volunteers to do the work and club subscription fees to cover running costs, it had been an uphill struggle.

'We were strapped for cash,' admitted WFA secretary Pat Gregory. 'We knew – well, some of us knew – there was opposition [to the WFA's independence], and we knew that in order to make it, enable it to develop, we had no choice. It had to go over to the FA. One thing that still rankles – with me, anyway – if we had had even a portion of the financial support earlier, how the scene might have changed!'

The funding that got put into women's football under the FA's auspices began to trickle in from 2011. In September 2008, the FA had finally announced their intention to launch a semi-professional, eight-team Women's Super League in the summer of 2010, which was subsequently delayed by a year. Initially a competition to run over the summer months, in the men's close season, players would receive some remuneration, buying them time to train, but probably not enough for a living wage. The idea of restricting the number of teams in the league to eight was to ensure that the talent was equally distributed and not too thinly spread, making a competitive league more likely – all the better to benefit the England national team set-up.

One of the unique features of the FA's new WSL, which made it very different to most other European leagues, male or female, was its club licensing system. Clubs had to apply to be a part of the inaugural season, and there was no need for a club to have a track record of playing success; indeed, the FA encouraged applications from newly created clubs. All applicants were required, however, to detail how they would meet specified benchmarks for financial and business management, commercial and marketing, facilities and playing and support staff.

Lincoln Ladies were one of the WSL's founder members. They had had a women's team since 1995, when they began playing regional football, and rose through the leagues to the FA Women's Premier League Northern Division – the second tier prior to the introduction of the WSL, just below the Women's National Premier League. In the seasons before the WSL's launch, Lincoln Ladies had become more and more closely associated with the men's club Lincoln City, wearing their kit and crest, and using their home stadium Sincil Bank. The two clubs shared a director in Ray Trew, who eventually left the City board in 2006, and went on to buy another men's team, Notts County, four years later while still backing Lincoln Ladies.

In the first two WSL seasons, Lincoln finished fourth, then fifth. The application process opened for the next licence to play in the WSL from 2014 onwards, and in April 2013, after one week of the third WSL season, it was announced that Lincoln had successfully applied for a place in the FAWSL 2014 as Notts County. Lincoln played the rest of the season out in their original home, with the average home crowd dropping from 526 in 2012 to 269 in 2013, and the team finishing sixth in the table. The final Lincoln Ladies match was the 2013 Continental Cup final where they lost 2–0 to Arsenal.

Rick Passmoor had taken the job as Lincoln manager after a swiftly arranged interview one New Year's Eve. He had been coaching in Leeds, got a phone call at 11 a.m., and drove down the A1 for a meeting with the club chairman at around 4.30 p.m. One week later, they rang back and made him an offer, which he agreed in principle immediately.

'That was good enough for me,' he said, before revealing that he got a voice message later that evening from a very big club in the women's game asking him if he would be interested in taking over there. 'I could have just turned around and said, "No, thanks, Lincoln, I'm going here." I did speak to the other club and I said, "I apologise, I've agreed."

'"Have you signed anything?"

'"No."

'"Come and speak to us."

'No, that's not me, because if I'm of that nature, how can I trust or have loyalty with my own staff and my own players?'

Unlike the fans – to whom the news came as a shock – Passmoor and his players were kept well informed about the plans to move Lincoln's franchise across the Midlands to Nottingham.

'We all knew, and all the players knew of the transfer,' he said, listing off the reasons why switching to Nottingham made sense. It was not just financial; it was the city's sporting history and facilities, plus two university campuses. 'Certainly it's a real proper city in terms of sport: the ice hockey, two football teams, Nottinghamshire cricket with Trent Bridge, and they play the England internationals there.'

Observers, however, were less convinced that it was a smart move. Dr Jo Welford, a football researcher based in the Midlands, kept a very close eye on what was happening and was very anxious that Lincoln may be making a mistake. She likened it to the controversial decision in the men's game to allow Wimbledon to move to Milton Keynes and rename themselves MK Dons, suggesting that Lincoln were keen to extend their fan base and attach themselves to a club which was offering them greater financial support.

'It wasn't a huge move distance-wise. We're talking 40, 50 miles, I think,' she said, 'but it was a complete rebranding of a team as a new team – some of the same players, but new kit, new ground, new identity for the club.'

Welford added that she thought there was a strong sense among women's football teams that they needed to be attached to a financially supportive men's club as a 'parent', and that those without the monetary backing would go under. With places in the WSL awarded by application for a licence which lasted for a limited number of seasons, it hardly required long-term strategic thinking.

'They only have to provide commitment for a certain period of time, and that gets reviewed,' she explained. 'Given the precarious financial position that a lot of men's clubs are in, outside of the [Premier League] top five or six, that is a big worry for women's clubs – as we know from other clubs that the women's team is often the first to go when there are financial troubles, despite them actually costing quite a small amount of their overall running costs.'

She was not surprised that Lincoln had been looking for another home, saying that women's teams at that point were not taken particularly seriously by many people, and despite the work of many people to boost its profile, it was struggling to carve out its niche.

'It [was] really bad for the local area,' she said. 'They [had] built up quite a committed fan base, and those fans [were] just going to be lost – you couldn't guarantee that they are going to travel 40, 50 miles. I think if people [watch] that level of football it's because it's local to them, it's easy for them to get to, it's not something they're going to start travelling huge distances to do.'

Passmoor was well aware of the challenges his side would continue to face, though, even in a bigger city with better transport connections and a good catchment area to attract new talent as well as new fans. In such a new league, players would sign one-year contracts, meaning that squad turnover was high and stability was low. With a relatively small talent pool and no centre of excellence attached to the club to allow young players to filter through, Passmoor had to work hard to get a skeleton squad together, let alone one that could compete to win matches in the WSL.

He also found his communication and pastoral care skills tested at Notts County as they began to attract good players who had lost their love for the game while in the hot-house environment of one of the big clubs in England or further afield.

'They needed polishing up,' he said. 'It was actually really like, "Well, we don't have the resources, we don't have the money, we don't have the facilities, why are you coming here?" And I think what it was to do with [was] the social attachment, how we managed the players, how we cared for them as people, and also they knew that the training would be of an elite level for them to develop and progress, which many did, but unfortunately for myself you were then juggling all the time.'

He meant that once players rediscovered their passion for football and benefited from the supportive environment and excellent standard of training, they were scouted by a big club; he pointed to England international Alex Greenwood's stellar 2015 season, which secured her a move to Liverpool, and later to Manchester United and European giants Lyon.

In December 2016, after almost a year on the market, Notts County – men's and women's – were purchased by a new owner, Alan Hardy. County had been due in court to face a winding-up petition from Her Majesty's Revenue and Customs, but it was adjourned to February 2017 and Hardy confirmed his aim to clear all the debts.

Passmoor had spoken to the chairman in 2015, and told him that what the club needed was to invest in structure and longevity, and to build facilities. Had Notts County followed his plan, he thought they would have been able to mirror the progress of the likes of Chelsea's Cobham set-up or Arsenal's London Colney or, on a smaller scale, Bristol City's Stoke Gifford complex. The resources simply were not there, and Passmoor felt that the club was being left behind.

'It was going to be a long, hard journey so I think after about 2016, I could see things changing within the club,' he said.

Trew, who had supported the team and the development of the women's side of the club, had decided to sell his stake and withdraw from football completely. Passmoor suspected that the men's team simply took priority, with the women's team getting shunted further and further down the track, and the finances becoming ever more stretched.

'I knew there was difficulties, because things were getting stripped back,' said Passmoor. Suddenly the team's training was switching locations with no notice, and he had no game analyst or scouts. He found himself taking on more and more of those backroom tasks himself, exhausting himself, and using up plenty of time he could have spent working with his squad.

'It was very, very difficult. I think unfortunately for ourselves, possibly the quick hits of finals [the 2015 Women's FA Cup final and the League Cup final], Wembley [for the FA Cup final], we might have made it too early, too soon. The club got to tick boxes that they'd done what they achieved.'

Chelsea Weston had joined the club at that point, having spent the years before that at Birmingham City, the team she supported. She was looking for a fresh start and the time and space to concentrate on rehabilitation after a string of injuries had hampered her progress. She knew Passmoor of old, as well as some of the Notts County players, and decided to give up her job as an accounts junior to give full-time football a try. She signed her deal in April 2016, and tore her anterior cruciate ligament in July. By December, salary payments were arriving late, and Weston – with her knowledge of accountancy – was unhappy with what that might mean.

In April 2017, Notts County were due to play Arsenal in the opening game of the Spring Series, an interim competition to fill the gap as the WSL switched from a summer league to the traditional winter calendar. On the Thursday evening prior to the match, the players were called into a meeting on the Friday morning, and had no idea what to expect.

'We all sat there,' she said. 'We were all laughing and joking, but actually there was a bit of "God, what's going on?"'

Weston had seen Passmoor walking down the stairs with his assistant manager Colin Walker just before the meeting started, and thought they both seemed distressed. 'At that point, the group were like, OK, this is not good now,' she said. 'And then what happened when we went in there was an utter disgrace.'

The squad were told by board members – whom Weston had not even met before – that the women's team was folding with immediate effect. 'We just got, "There's no club no more, you've got no job,"' she said. 'Just like that.'

The players left the building to be met by television camera crews, who had been tipped off about the news before they had even had an inkling. Some of the squad had mortgages and were shocked to find they now had no regular income to pay those bills. Weston had just bought a new car, and was sharing a house with team-mates, with most of the costs covered by the club; that too was about to be withdrawn, and they were asked to depart before the end of May. Weston decided to stay on for the next few weeks as she continued her rehab, but her house-mates Jo Potter and Jade Moore left to sign for Reading, with their fourth housemate and Irish international Louise Quinn joining Arsenal.

Left alone, Weston decided to go back home. 'Luckily I had family to go home to, but what was I going home to? I had no job. I had nothing.'

County issued a club statement, which was clear: 'Alan Hardy has reluctantly admitted defeat in his bid to save Notts County Ladies Football Club after facing a near-£1m bill to keep the club afloat this season . . . Despite weeks of negotiations with lawyers, HMRC and the Football Association, Hardy has now called time on his plans to save the Ladies' set-up. The club has today been officially withdrawn from the Women's Super League and will play no matches in the Spring Series, including this Sunday's away fixture at Arsenal.'

Quinn had gone into the meeting with some nerves. She thought that the announcement that training was cancelled at such short notice had to augur very badly for the team. 'You don't cancel training,' she said. 'You postpone it, you move it, you change to a different time. You don't cancel training.'

She had only been at County for a matter of weeks, and many of her team-mates were concerned for her, having moved her life over to England and then to lose her job like that. Quinn, however, considered herself one of the luckier ones when the news broke.

'It was really heart-breaking to be in the room [for the meeting],' she said. 'Some of the other girls felt sorry for me because I'd just arrived. I felt more for them – they were settled, some had houses or apartments or were studying or had their partners there. I had a couple of suitcases and a car, and I'd actually just brought my car over from Ireland, literally a couple of weeks earlier, so I was really, really lucky. Then I got really lucky that within a few hours I had a team.'

Quinn's move to Arsenal happened very quickly. Gunners manager Pedro Martínez Losa had been interested in signing her previously but nothing had been agreed, but he moved fast when she became available again.

'We finally found that out on a Friday morning and by Friday evening I had already been told that Arsenal wanted me to be training there for Saturday or Sunday,' she said. 'It obviously started flooding out that Notts County had folded. As players we were quite concerned because you know the transfer windows had closed, and there were Euros coming up in the summer. The girls that were in that were like, "What the hell are we going to do?"

'Thankfully the FA just opened the window. It was definitely more helpful that it was only the Spring Series – something to carry over [rather than a full season].'

The fans saw the whole drama unfold via social media as the players began to post about the club's closure – midfielder Dani Buet's tweet that she was 'jobless and homeless' struck a chord with many. Supporters tried to organise crowdfunding to create a fund that the players who had suddenly lost their income and accommodation could draw upon.

'We didn't get much feedback off it – women's football is really low on people's scale, unfortunately,' said Julie Roberts, from Newark, in Lincolnshire. She had been a passionate supporter of Lincoln Ladies and followed them to Notts County. Coming from the world of rugby league, she wanted to bring some of that type of fan culture to women's football, and set up an official supporters' club. They ran fundraising events, and also put on coaches to take fans to away games that were further afield, enabling them to support the team wherever they played.

She heard some whispers that something was happening with regard to the club's future, and when confirmation came, it was tough to accept. 'It was like a family member had died. It was absolutely awful,' she said.

Something good did come out of Roberts' love for the team – she qualified as a Level 1 football coach, and since then has been able to work with a local club. 'I love coaching,' she enthused. 'Because Notts County were my team, it was like a family, and I thought, "I'm never ever going to watch a women's football team again," and then this advert came up in Newark saying, "We're after a coach and a manager," and I went for it, and I've got my little family back.'

Although the fans' crowdfunding had been unsuccessful, the union was able to provide some assistance. The Professional Footballers' Association stepped in to support Weston and her team-mates where required. Weston was in a particularly tough spot knowing that an injured player was unlikely to get another club quickly.

'I was still coming back from my ACL [injury], and nobody wants you,' she said. 'That's a side of football . . . I understand it, but at the same time, that's where you don't get looked after as a person. If the PFA hadn't been there to help me financially, I don't even know what I'd be doing now.'

After spells in the semi-professional Championship, Weston had moved abroad to ply her trade in Italy, and had taken steps to protect her future. 'Football doesn't care about you,' she said, reflecting on her bad luck and string of serious injuries. She had worked in a string of varied jobs, but looking ahead, she had enrolled in a graphic design degree. 'So hopefully come the end of my career, I'll have something to go into, so fingers crossed that works out.'

Conversely, her former housemate Louise Quinn wondered whether Notts County's closure was actually the most fortunate event of her career. She enjoyed great success with Arsenal, winning the 2018/19 FA WSL title there under new manager Joe Montemurro, who replaced Losa in November 2017, a few months after Quinn signed for the club.

'It's silver linings completely,' she said. 'To me, it really was the best thing that could have happened. I was extremely lucky. Even at that stage it was tough adapting to England as well for me at the time – a completely different pace of the game, different skills, a different set-up. Even the pitches that we trained on [at Notts County] really weren't great. We were training on what was like a Sunday League pitch – when it was warm, it was rock solid, and if it rained a little bit it was a mud bath. And within a few days I was on the carpet of Arsenal – a real, real turnaround.'

Passmoor had been working in the men's game ever since leaving Notts County, and was wary of returning to manage a women's team in the future.

'Notts County was a challenge and it was definitely an experience,' he said, 'and I do think that potentially a younger coach or [one] less experienced would have found it even more difficult, and may have moved on earlier. Going forward with any return to the women's game, there would be a lot more due diligence and a lot more thought process into the club's vision, their own culture.'

Thinking back on his loud encouragement of his team on the touchline, he added wryly: 'I didn't mean to be that loud and under pressure on the sidelines. If I ever get the opportunity to come back, people will be quite surprised, I might be a bit quieter!'

TWELVE

THE FOUND

NOTTS COUNTY'S DEMISE GAVE DEFENDER Shelly Provan the impetus to make some changes in her life – most notably coming to the decision to have her second child. She and husband Callum already had a two-year-old son, and they thought that without football commitments it would be a good time to add to their family.

Provan and her husband were both working as PE teachers in the same school in Romsey, Hampshire. She had always balanced her day job with football, and had always been based in or near Southampton. She spent a matter of months with Notts County, but before that she turned out for Reading and for Doncaster Belles, commuting up and down the country for training and for matches. It involved a lot of travel, some expenses that barely covered her petrol costs, and very little sleep.

'When Super League 1 initially started [in 2011], I signed for Doncaster Belles and I was full-time at school – I was a full-time teacher,' she said. 'I'd literally park my car outside the school for three o'clock, leave, I'd get in the car, drive to Nottingham, I'd meet a few of the players . . . we drove from Nottingham up to Doncaster for a seven o'clock start [of training].

'I was seeing a guy who was in the army, who was based in Nottingham, and I used to drive back to Nottingham in the evening, stay over and leave at about five o'clock in the morning to drive back from Nottingham for a half eight start [at school]. I used to do that twice during the week, and then for games on Sunday. That was the reality. I don't think people saw that. That's what girls did to be a part of what was happening, and I was so determined to be a part of what was happening, that's the lengths we went to just to be a part of it.

'I look back now and the whole recovery, sport science side of things is just crazy. When I got up at five o'clock I'd be drinking Red Bull on the way down to Romsey, down to Southampton, trying to keep myself awake. Everybody who played in those times can tell the same stories, opening their windows, music on loud, just trying to keep yourself awake because you were travelling so much. There were late nights all over the place. I know everybody of my era went through that, but I think that shows the character of the girls who did play at that level.'

She considered relocation every so often, and had been offered jobs within clubs alongside her playing contract, but the security of teaching was too much for her to give up for something that could be a huge financial risk. Before signing for Belles, she had been with Bristol Academy when the WSL first launched. She knew she would not be part of manager Mark Sampson's plans, and she was not in a position to take up one of the professional contracts on offer; the money available was too little compared to her solid teaching salary.

'It's great for girls that are finishing college or finishing uni, they can afford to be paid 11 grand a year, and I knew I wasn't going to be one of those people,' she said. 'That was probably the hardest thing, knowing the club that I was at was going into that system, but he didn't want me to be part of that. The thought of going somewhere else was the only thing on my mind, and I think that's why I ended up committing so much with Doncaster Belles, because I wanted to be a part of it, and it was finding a way and a club to do that.'

She left Belles to sign for Reading, then managed by a former team-mate of hers, Jayne Ludlow, whose assistant Kelly

Chambers invited her to join the Royals. 'Kelly approached me and asked me to go to Reading and said that Jayne was coming in to be manager, and I was really pleased with that, actually, really pleased,' she said. 'She's a fantastic coach, a fantastic person. The difference with her was that she had a lot of confidence in me, and I knew that, and I think that's probably why I had one of my better seasons that I've had, just because I knew that she rated me, and that was huge for me.'

At the start of 2017, after being released from Reading, Provan had agreed to sign for Notts County for the Spring Series campaign. She was reunited with players she knew from age-group international football, such as England stars Laura Bassett and Carly Telford.

'I was quite excited to be part of that,' Provan recalled. 'I almost felt like I wasn't worthy at the time. I think I'd had a couple of good performances against them for Reading, and the manager [Rick Passmoor] said he'd been tracking me for a while, and it was a position they needed and he was keen for me to sign. At that point I was feeling a bit negative about football, I'd been released from Reading and I wasn't sure whether I wanted to carry on or not, and that was the pick-me-up I needed to carry on.'

On arrival, Provan was aware very quickly that there were financial issues at the club and its future was looking shaky; when the hammer fell and the team folded, she felt grateful that she had not uprooted her life or given up her teaching job to move there, but was concerned for her team-mates. Because she was at work, she was not even at the club when the players were called to that meeting and the news broken.

'All the other girls were full-time, they were living in Nottingham, they'd built their lives there, so I was probably lucky in that again, for me, another good decision was that I hadn't quit my job to go and do that, because this is what happens, you know? It's not secure.

'I felt so sorry for the girls that it did happen to. You could tell that they were genuinely distraught by what had happened there. They were happy there, they were settled – it must have been a huge thing for them.'

Even though Notts County folded, Provan was sanguine; these things happened in football, especially women's football, and she knew she would never be a superstar that clubs were fighting over to offer huge money.

'I've always worked really hard to be there, probably punched above my weight at the clubs that I have been [at], just because I've grafted so much,' she said. 'I think sometimes they'd find better players . . . definitely at Bristol I think there was a player that came in that they felt was stronger than me, at Doncaster it was more about the financial side, I think, in the end, and then I went to Reading, so I never thought about location.

'I look back and say there were reasons why I wasn't performing as well as I probably could, because I was trying to keep my job going and keep myself playing the best I could. I don't make excuses for that. Managers have decisions they have to make.'

So without a club to play for, it seemed the ideal time to add to her family. Then the phone rang. It was a coach who Provan had worked with in the England set-up who was now involved with Southampton FC Women.

Women's football in Southampton has a confusing history. Southampton Women FC's glory years of the 1970s and early 1980s, spearheaded by Sue Lopez and Pat Chapman, saw them win the Women's FA Cup eight times.

Red Star Southampton were founded in 1979, progressing through the Southern Regions League to join the FA Women's Premier League National Division when it was founded in

1991. They made an impressive start to life in the top echelon of domestic football, finishing second in the league and runners-up in the Women's FA Cup, losing out to Doncaster Belles in both competitions. However, they were relegated back to the Southern Premier League in 1995, and at that point Southampton FC – the men's club – took them under their wing, changing their name to Southampton Saints, and folding them into the set-up formally in 2001. Four years later, the men's team were relegated from the Premier League, suffering the usual financial impact, and cut Saints adrift as a result. Since then, Saints have re-established themselves as an independent club.

'It was Southampton Women to start with. They evolved, a lot of the players went to Red Star Southampton, and then they turned into Southampton Saints,' summarised Vanessa Raynbird. She had been associated with Southampton Women since 1980, as player and manager, and had been there for much of the city's tangled footballing history. She won the FA Cup in her first season as a player there, and it remained one of her fondest footballing memories.

'It is something that I really treasure – it's actually out on display now as we speak, the only medal I keep out, really, on display,' she said. 'We were playing with absolutely fantastic players. When I went there I was playing with the likes of Lynda Hale and Maggie Pearce – or Kirkland at the time – and Pat Chapman, Sue Lopez, Sue Buckett. Really almost everybody in that team represented their country . . . the majority were representing England, and it was brilliant, to be able to play amongst players of that calibre.'

Raynbird stopped playing when she was 39, and had never considered going into coaching – or even led a session – until the club chairman of the Southampton Saints asked if she would be interested in taking on the reserves. She took her Level One coaching badge, and led the reserves to the league title that year, and with Southampton Saints going through one of their times of massive turnover and change, she was invited to lead the first team the following season. She admitted she was a tough coach, focused on fitness and never letting her teams flag before the final whistle.

'I always thought that if you weren't fit enough, then you're not going to sustain the game, and your agility and any other part of your physical sort of prowess in the game would not excel unless you were fit,' she said. Her Saints team – then aligned loosely with the men's club – were allowed to use the sports hall next to their stadium, the Dell, one night a week for their fitness training. 'We would do circuit training, we would do shuttle runs, and it's all things they probably never do these days, but for me it was something that got them in the right shape and the right frame of mind to address a game. That was something I like to think that we did pretty well at – we didn't normally fade in games, we were normally pretty good to the end, and I think a lot goes down to that and the commitment level that people show when they are doing that sort of training.'

Of course, Raynbird's Southampton Saints were amateurs, still fundamentally organising themselves. After ten years of her tenure, and after a sixth-place finish in the National Division, the men's club came to the women's team with an offer of funding for the women's section. That was dependent on accepting that they would also put their own selection of staff in place and the women's team would be run by the men's club. Raynbird was not in a position to be considered as a potential Southampton employee; she had a full-time job at a company where she had been working for years, and even if she had been offered the women's team-manager role under the auspices of the men's club, she would not have taken it. She was offered a scouting job, but she was not interested in doing that.

So Raynbird left the club with which she had had such a happy association for so many years, and was sad and disappointed to have to do so. 'What a kick in the teeth,' she recalled. 'We'd progressed this club . . . and we'd worked really hard with the team over the years.'

Raynbird's next position was a switch across the south coast to Southampton's great rivals, Portsmouth, where she stayed for another ten years. She also took up a position with the Hampshire FA, sitting on the women's and girls' committee – and returned to the pitch with some Southampton team-mates, trying out the slower-paced walking football as a squad.

'We call ourselves the Ex-Saints!' she revealed. 'We do let the odd one in that wasn't. But there's lots of people there that would have represented in one guise or another, whether it be Red Star Southampton, Southampton Saints or Southampton Women. It's great to see all the girls again and we have a good old catch-up and we still play some decent stuff, as you can imagine.'

Southampton FC Women are the team now affiliated to Southampton FC, the Premier League men's club. After the success of the FA WSL and the bronze medal won by England's Lionesses at the Women's World Cup in Canada in 2015, many men's clubs began to realise they ought to be investing in women's football. In 2016, Southampton FC started to set up girls' and youth age-group sides within their Regional Talent Centre, and a year later, Provan got that call to invite her into the club to see what they had to offer.

Provan loved the idea of returning to the club with which she had been linked as a junior, but feared that they would want to set up an under-23 side and only be interested in her passing on her experience.

'I thought she was going to ask me to help coach, and I'm still not at that point!' said Provan. 'Even though I teach sport,

I don't think coaching is something that I want to go into until I finish the game. I remember saying to my husband, "She's going to ask me to coach, and I can't say no to her!" so I was really worried about the meeting. I was thinking, "I've got to be strong, I've got to be strong, I don't want to coach, I still want to play, I still want to play after I've had [the new baby]," and luckily she said, "Would you like to be one of our over-age players in the under-23s?" The relief was amazing! "She wants me to play!"'

Southampton then made a marquee appointment in the summer of 2018 when Marieanne Spacey – now known as Marieanne Spacey-Cale – was announced as their head of women's and girls' football. Famous as a player for her time with Arsenal and England, Spacey-Cale had left her position as the national team's assistant coach to head up the Southampton women's division. A few months previously, Southampton had announced that they were bidding for a licence to play in the FA Women's Championship, but were ultimately unsuccessful, despite there being five vacancies in the league. At that point, though, Southampton did not have a senior women's team – just the sides in the age-group set-up. Spacey-Cale's first task was to pull together a senior squad to play in the 2018/19 Southern Region Premier Division.

They proceeded to win 18 games on the spin, securing promotion to the National League Division One. Provan watched with interest and envy during her maternity break. She might not have been able to play in the immediate future, but Southampton took care of her from the off, providing her with a training plan during her pregnancy. She had already had experience of returning to the pitch with Reading after giving birth to her son, but this time round with Southampton and her daughter it was a real contrast.

'When I had Austin, I'd had probably my most enjoyable season of football under Jayne Ludlow at Reading, when they were in Super League 2,' she said. 'I'd just had a really consistent season, really enjoyed being at the club, and then just before pre-season found out I was pregnant with Austin. The season that I was out whilst I was pregnant, they got promoted, so when I came back not only was I coming back from having a child, I was coming back into a team that was going up into the league above, so for me it was my challenge to get back.

'I just enjoyed that season so much, I wanted to be a part of what was happening with the promotion. It's probably wholly my mentality, that's probably the way I've always been. Nobody was surprised that was the way I did it. They'd say, "Are you sure you're OK, how are you feeling?" It's hard when you haven't got that specific knowledge on getting back. Even on the internet it's really hard – there's loads more now – I found myself googling what you can do, what you can't do. There was so little information out there to guide me, I just went on how I felt, really.'

Provan was quick to acknowledge the support of her husband Callum, who took on more than his share of the childcare along with his full-time job – as her head of department. 'Even though I see him lots during the day, we don't necessarily have quality time together, but at least we get to see each other during the day when we're at work!'

'He's fantastic – he's probably the sole reason I am able to do what I do and I have been able to since I've had the children,' she said. On the three nights when Provan had training at Southampton, he collected the children from nursery and did the evening routine as well as looking after them on game days. She was working three days a week and looking after little Evie at home for the other two school days.

Provan sustained a serious injury in training in 2019, tearing her anterior cruciate ligament, but Southampton's care and support was impressive. She had access to exactly the same kind of treatment and rehabilitation that any of the men's first team would have had.

'I look back and I think if I'd have been at any other club, whether I was in the Super League 1, Super League 2, I don't think any of those clubs would have been able to give me the support that Southampton have. I was getting access to the men's physios – they were all bouncing off each other, they were making decisions based on what I wanted long-term, short-term, they were taking into consideration how long I wanted to play for, what sort of activity I wanted to do in 15, 20 years' time. It wasn't just like, "How quickly can we get you back on the pitch?" It was, "As a person and a player, what is best for you?" I don't think any of the other clubs that I've been at would have been able to do that. As much as I've worked with some fantastic people and lovely people, it's nowhere near the level that I've experienced at Southampton for sure.'

Of course, the injury and the rehab also meant that Provan could not go to her day job either. The surgeon who operated on the ligament signed her off work for four months, giving her time to go into the training ground most days to work on her rehab. Southampton sent taxis to pick her up and drop her off as she was unable to drive.

'Literally everything was thought of,' she said, 'so when I went back to work, it was a case of just changing round the times I did my rehab, but it worked out fine. I'd go in in the evenings: I'd go after work and do my rehab in the evening. By that point I was comfortable enough to do my job, it's an active job. I think they were very conscious of that. That's why I was signed off for the length of time I was, and I was fully paid as a result, which was great, so I was really lucky. I know others who have gone through very different situations with the same injury.'

Southampton were in the FA Women's National League Division One South West, the feeder league for the FA

Women's National League Premier Division South. Winning that could give them a chance of promotion to the FA Women's Championship, so they were still quite some way from the top of the game and being on par with the fully professional sides. Former Arsenal manager Vic Akers had watched his old player Spacey shape her Southampton set-up, and thought what she was building looked very familiar, in the most positive of ways.

'We [at Arsenal] started to create a team and developed a team that was good enough to go through the leagues, a similar scenario to what Marieanne Spacey is doing at Southampton, because I see her success,' reflected Akers. 'I speak to Marieanne on a regular basis, and I see the Arsenal in Southampton as it were, although Southampton Ladies were one of the biggest clubs – I know the ladies who organised that as well. That Marieanne's now taken on the form of Southampton Football Club to enhance the scenario that we had, she probably sees the same thing in what we did as to what she's doing down there, although probably on a bigger scale – they're more involved with the club in terms of facilities and things like that. I've been down to the club itself and seen the facilities they work in, with Marieanne. It's first-class. They're going to be a force in the next five to ten years.'

Provan – who could be forgiven for fretting over any club's financial future after her experiences – too was reassured by Southampton's commitment to the team.

'When I was at Southampton as a youngster and we were in the National League, it coincided with when the men got relegated,' she explained. 'That's when the money came out of the women's side – we always knew that, and I think clubs will always worry about that. I think we're lucky at Southampton that their commitment to us is huge, and it's a long-term commitment no matter what, but I don't think it's the same at every club.'

In March 2021, due to the coronavirus pandemic, the women's leagues from the third tier downwards were brought to a close for the second successive season. However, clubs were invited to apply for the euphemistically called 'upward movement' – or promotion by any other name. Southampton FC Women had been at the top of the FA Women's National League Division One South West for the two previous years having not lost a game; it was not a surprise that their elevation to the next tier up was confirmed, particularly as three-quarters of the application was weighted towards on-the-pitch performance.

After Southampton legend Sue Lopez retired from playing, she compiled a history of the game. *Women on the Ball* is still the most accessible and authoritative account of the way female footballers kept their own sport running for decades.

Lopez – never entirely happy speaking to the media – gave a rare interview to the *Daily Telegraph* in 2020, from her nursing home in Hampshire. Three years previously, she had been diagnosed with dementia, like so many of the high-profile male footballers of her generation. Lopez attributed her illness to all the heading of the heavy leather ball she did as a player, acknowledging that she had suffered headaches and concussions throughout her career which she thought would have contributed.

Although work is still being done in the area to establish the causes, current research from experts at the University of Glasgow has indicated that former professional footballers are three and a half times more likely to die with dementia than those who did not play.

Lisa Savage, appointed in 2021 as Southampton FC's coach development lead for the women's and girls' programme, named Lopez as one of her mentors and inspirations. The two had met when Savage had a trial for Lopez's Saints squad, and ended up joining the reserves. Savage admired the way that Lopez integrated players across the first-team and reserve set-ups, allowing players to step up if required.

Coaching was never on Savage's radar; it had never occurred to her as a possible opportunity, and she was so dedicated to playing she did not look at any other way to be involved in football.

'I remember watching [Lopez] take some sessions and I thought, "This is actually quite good!"' she recalled. 'Prior to that I played for other teams, and we did have a coach and sometimes it was a serious coach, sometimes we just turned up and had a kickabout. This just seemed to have a little bit more structure to it, more professionalism to it.

'We'd stand back and watch how she would deliver sessions and her terminology that she'd be using, and I'd never met another female coach.'

When people talk about role models in women's football, one particular phrase crops up again and again: 'You have to see it to be it.' It might be becoming a cliché, but that was how Savage felt when she saw Lopez coach; she realised that coaching was an option for women, and so was working in football full-time.

Savage was working as a gardener and combining that tough physical work with football, training three times a week and playing a match at the weekend. When she suffered a back injury, she needed to reconsider her job and her leisure activity, both of which she loved dearly, which took a toll mentally as well. It was Lopez who supported her, checking in to ensure she was coping, and then offering her the chance to get involved with coaching when it transpired that her fitness would not bounce back to the level required to play regularly.

'She just said, "Do you want to come along and start doing some coaching?" I was like, "I don't know, really, to be honest!" That was genuinely my first reaction – not to be ungrateful, [but] I didn't want to wear the captain's armband. I didn't want to coach, all I wanted to do was play football and score goals, that was literally all I wanted to do.'

Savage agreed to go along to a session and just observe from the sidelines, rather than throwing herself headlong into coaching immediately. Then she went to some more, seeing how training sessions changed and varied according to the age group, and spent a year finding her feet as a coach. Southampton Women – one of the other clubs in the area – invited her to join them as a coach, and she stayed there for several seasons, turning into a mentor for novice coaches herself, but still asking Lopez for advice when needed.

'What I did take from her actually was her interpersonal skills . . . the way she would speak to players, and there was never any kind of anger, from what I saw; it was always just quite a calm approach and just being open and honest and upfront with you,' said Savage, who added that she tried to imitate that approach, being open with her players and always having firm and sound reasoning behind every decision.

'In terms of coaching style, I didn't necessarily adopt her style – not because I didn't agree with it, just purely because my personality is very different to her personality, so I started to find my own coaching style, my own coaching behaviours, which is why now I've been fortunate enough to go on and tutor coaching qualifications [since 2016] and be an FA mentor [since 2014].'

Savage returned to Southampton FC Women as technical coach for the B team, and then stepped in to assist Marieanne Spacey-Cale with the first team, before moving over to lead the foundation phase in the girls' regional talent centre programme, and then taking on the coach development route in the summer of 2021. Encouraging new talent through the ranks had slowly become her passion, unconsciously following in the footsteps of people like Lopez, who had guided her along her own coaching pathway.

'Now I'm going down the coach development route, which is a brand new role as well – the club have created this role in the women's and girls' programme. It's very common in the men's and boys' programmes, but now they've created this role, a part-time role at the moment, and I'm looking forward to working with the fantastic coaches that we have there.

'I've never expected anybody to be like me. I don't want that. Be the best version of you, do things your way.'

EPILOGUE – THE FUTURE

IN SEPTEMBER 2018, THE FA Women's Super League turned fully professional for the very first time. The definition of this professionalisation was for all the players at top-flight clubs to get a minimum of 16 contact hours per week. In contrast, the clubs in the semi-professional FA Women's Championship were still only required to provide eight hours of contact time – but naturally any club with ambition was already signing up players who would be considered 'full-time' under this definition, all the better to push for promotion to the elite.

Former England striker Karen Farley was no longer involved in football at all. She returned to England from Sweden in 2005, met her partner, and settled down to raise their family – a son and a daughter.

'I've had countless people, local to where I live, say, "Oh, can you come and run the kids' team? Can you do this?" But I somehow gave birth to a son who couldn't be more uninterested in football. It's hilarious. He couldn't give a hoot. Our daughter is a little bit more interested but not really. So they're like, "Come on, coach the team! You'd be brilliant!" and I'm like, "No, I can't spend all my spare time coaching other people's kids when my children will be sitting at home – they're my priority."

'If Noah was to suddenly turn around and say, "Mum, I really want to play football!" or Poppy were to, then I'd be like,

"Yeah, absolutely awesome!" and then I'll get involved, but now it's the turn for my family to come first.'

Of course, being a footballer meant that if there was a game on, she would watch it, and she had helped out a friend who was in charge of a local children's team. What did concern her was the win-at-all-costs mentality she was seeing even at very young age groups, with the adults fretting about what potential scouts from professional clubs might think or say, and the players themselves throwing tantrums, demanding the ball, and generally copying unpleasant gamesmanship they might have seen on television. Farley's attitude towards all levels of football was shaped by the influence of the legendary coach Pia Sundhage, famous for her time in charge of the USA national team.

'She was my coach in Sweden for many years, and she would never let us train without a football at our feet,' Farley recalled. 'She was like, "We are footballers, and we are enjoying our football – you can get fit with a football at your feet," and doing little drills with the balls involved.

'And she always said, "Have fun." Those were always the last words she said to us before we went out for a game. 'Have fun.' Remember this, remember that, but remember the most important thing – have fun – because that is why you do it. And of course you want to win, and of course it's terrible when you lose, but you've got to be able to lose. You've got to be able to look at a team, and think, "They were better than us today, and so what are they doing that I'm not doing? What is that player there doing that I'm not doing, which meant that she was better than me?"

'I don't go to matches personally, but, yeah, I do watch them, I like watching the women's football,' said Sheila Parker, the first-ever England captain, and one of the women who had blazed the trail for the much-lauded Lionesses of the 21st century to follow. 'But to me, the sport . . . to me, the sport's changed. It's not like it used to be.'

In what way?

'Money. End of subject.'

'Of course, at the end of the day, the football that you're seeing in the women's game has moved on to tremendous levels,' said Vic Akers, the former Arsenal manager. 'The one thing that was always a problem in women's football was goalkeeping. Nowadays there's massive improvement in that area as well, which it needed to be, if we were going to be professional – we had to make sure that there were people doing actual goalkeeping coaching individuals, because it is an individual sector. So it needed to improve twofold and it has, and right along the line, everything is improved for the girls. And I'm delighted – although I'm disappointed I never got that sort of money in my time.'

'I've always said I was born too soon,' said Gill Sayell, one of his first-ever Arsenal players. 'As I was finishing playing, that was when it all started to take off – the Women's Premier League, the FA were really involved in taking it on. It was just starting to move places. I loved it, playing in the way we did and when we did, the school of hard knocks, coming through and playing on really dire pitches.

'I'm just so pleased it's progressed, albeit slowly. It should have taken off when we came back from Mexico – that was a good springboard, because the ban was lifted. We'd like to think maybe we were a little bit instrumental in that happening. Maybe it would have happened anyway. We don't know. It's all part of it – all part of the tapestry of the history of women's football, I suppose.'

Karen Farley built herself a den in her back garden where she displayed all her football memorabilia. When people asked her if she would have wanted to be born two decades later to reap all the benefits – and money – of professionalisation, she said no.

'You know what? I loved it when we played, because we all did it purely for the love of football,' she said. 'We stayed with our teams because we were loyal to our teams. There was no money involved, there was no transfer fee or someone offering you more money. There was nothing like that, so it was purely about football and about your team-mates, and just about the fun that we had and about how much we all loved it.

'And that's not saying that the girls today don't love it but they've got a different reality that they're living in. It's not just about those 90 minutes on the pitch, and the training. It's all of the media coverage and the sponsorships and all those sorts of things.'

March 2019 saw the biggest ever financial investment into women's football in England via a corporate partner – indeed, women's sport in the UK as a whole – as the FA announced that Barclays would sponsor the Women's Super League domestic competition for the next three years. The bank gave its name to the league as well as several million pounds to the game.

It was an impressive figure to add to the top flight's coffers, guaranteeing an increased marketing spend to promote the league, but also bringing in a new annual £500,000 prize fund to be distributed according to clubs' final league position.

The new partners were also quick to say the investment would benefit the game's grassroots as well. Barclays also became the lead partner of the FA Girls' Football School Partnerships, a nationwide scheme to help develop girls' access to football, with hubs across the country delivering programmes in schools. Kelly Simmons, the FA's director for the women's professional game, said in a press release at the time that the link-up with schools was 'a cornerstone to our ambition to double participation within The FA's Gameplan for Growth strategy and will see girls across the country given the opportunity to begin a relationship with football, which we hope will last a lifetime.'

Jes Staley, Group CEO of Barclays, added in the same statement: 'Our commitment to women's and girls' football, at a crucial time in its development, goes beyond pure sponsorship – we believe it can be a key to increasing participation, development and the wider visibility of the female game.'

It was an exciting announcement – a multi-million-pound deal for Europe's only fully professional domestic female football league – and came just a few months before the Women's World Cup in France, where Phil Neville's England side were expected to do well. Indeed, the success of the Lionesses was pivotal to the Gameplan for Growth strategy Simmons mentioned – a four-year strategy announced in 2017 with the aims of doubling women's and girls' participation in football, doubling the fanbase for the women's game, and creating a high-performance system for England teams.

Despite their high-profile manager and the wide media coverage of their campaign, England only finished fourth in France – no medal, and going one worse than they had managed four years previously, when much of the WSL was still semi-professional, and without the sizeable financial injection. Nevertheless, the interest in the top tier of the women's game continued, and after several years of fans grumbling about their lack of access to televised matches, the FA Player gave viewers the opportunity to stream and watch again almost every fixture from the WSL and the FA Women's Championship. Then almost two years to the day after the Barclays sponsorship was announced, in the spring of 2021 a new deal with broadcasters was revealed – the first time broadcast rights for the women's game in England had been sold separately from the men's. The BBC, the national broadcaster, confirmed they would be showing 22 live games per season, with a minimum of 18 matches on their mainstream, free-to-air channels, BBC One and BBC Two, rather than on BBC iPlayer or the BBC Red Button, as they had been previously. Alongside that, Sky Sports paid for the right to show up to 44 matches, with at least 35 of them being screened across their premium channels Sky Sports Main Event, Sky Sports Premier League and Sky Sports Football, with some matches also shown simultaneously on their freeview stations Sky Sports Mix and Sky One.

Rick Passmoor, the former Notts County manager, watched the progress of the women's game with interest but also a certain amount of caution. 'We're still in our infancy – the male game is 130 years old, we're not even a decade into professionalism,' he reflected prior to the announcement of that broadcast deal. 'What we can't do is self-implode. We need to concentrate on the good things, because the game is still, well, not quicksand, but it still hasn't got across the board a complete foundation.'

A constant refrain from the players of the past was that the first generation of fully professional female footballers in England were athletes, rather than great with a ball.

'I've watched women's football on TV now,' said Vicky Johnson, winner of the Women's FA Cup with Lowestoft Town, 'and the standard of the football, to me, isn't as high as what Lowestoft were playing. It's not because I'm biased because I played at that time. Generally as a football fan, I would say that Lowestoft Town Ladies' standard of football was slightly higher than what's being played by the Man Cities and Chelseas and the Arsenals of today.'

Vic Akers, in his seventies, had stepped back from football, although he had recently done some scouting work for one of his old first-team coaches – Emma Hayes, now a very success-ful manager in charge of Chelsea Women. He still watched Arsenal, and admired many of their players, naming Dutch striker Vivianne Miedema as one who had particularly impressed him – but he also thought that many of his squads boasted players just as good.

'I had people in my team that if they'd played in [the] present day would have been unbelievable,' he asserted. 'Marieanne Spacey, going way back. Debbie Bampton, going way back. Julie Fleeting, who was a phenomenal, phenomenal goalscorer for Scotland.

'Thierry Henry also said to me one day: "The girl Kelly Smith . . . she's the one girl player I think could make it in men's football." That's an unbelievable statement. She was overwhelmed. That was a true fact.'

'We were natural players, because we didn't have what they've got,' said Pat Chapman, the Southampton goalscoring sensation. 'So we actually had to be natural players. You know, no one taught Brenda [Sempare] to do anything. She was just a born natural. You know? Lynda Hale the same. Sue Buckett – best goalkeeper ever. Pat Davies – best header of the ball I have ever seen. Liz Deighan, again, natural player, an absolutely natural player.'

Chapman was concerned that journalists and broadcasters continued to ignore decades of women's football history, even as they started to acknowledge the predecessors of the WSL. 'I listen to the commentators and I follow football,' she said, 'and they talk about players that played ten years ago as being the trailblazers. They're not. The trailblazers are the people much earlier than them.'

Carol Thomas agreed. 'I think it's nice that people are trying to get our era back into the limelight. I think we could have had more appreciation when we were playing . . . but if it's getting us back into the spotlight now I'm all for it. I think a lot of younger players today, certainly ones that I've heard speak, don't think that ladies' football started until the 1990s to be completely honest. That's a bit disappointing. That's one of the reasons I don't really watch a lot of the women's game at the moment.'

Indeed, it seemed to many as if anything that happened prior to the launch of the FA WSL had had a veil discreetly drawn over it, and its history carefully brushed aside, edited and used only when helpful. The FA was proud to launch its WSL Hall of Fame after a decade of competition, honouring the players who had shone since the introduction of official semi-professional and professional contracts, but by definition those who played prior to that cut-off point were excluded. The Hall of Fame's selection panel included FA staff, football journalists, and, with a nod to the past, named three former players, praising them as pioneers – Southampton FC Women head coach and former England assistant Marieanne Spacey-Cale, Brighton and Hove Albion Women head coach and former national team manager Hope Powell, and England junior coach and former central defender Mary Phillip. All had retired as players prior to the start of the WSL, with Powell and Spacey's careers extending back to the start of the 1980s, although both were probably at their peaks in the early 1990s; they had spent their domestic careers playing for clubs in London, apart from Spacey's spells overseas. There were no representatives from earlier playing eras, and nor were there significant representatives of some of the great clubs in women's football history – Southampton Women, for example, Fodens or Doncaster Belles.

Gill Coultard thought that the often-aired complaint that women's football had not been competitive until the introduction of the FA WSL was a little unfair – but she did think that some of the facilities available to modern players had enabled them to improve their game beyond what previous generations had achieved.

'Things have changed with the state of the pitches now,' she pointed out. 'We were playing with pitches that had no grass, playing in mud baths to play football, whereas now they're like carpets, aren't they? Things like that do change, but the competitiveness was part of my game. I'm very competitive. I look at myself now and I look at players that I would model myself on now; [the] likes of Jordan Nobbs, Fara Williams, even Rachel Furnesses are just as competitive as I am, so I don't think any of that has changed.

'I think as well from a technical point, ability, I don't think that's changed either – I just think things in and around the game have changed. Things have progressed with fitness levels, they're totally different, diet is totally different, the environment of women's football is totally different to what our era was, just like that era was totally different to the one before, with Dick, Kerr Ladies – that's totally different, it was a lot slower.'

'I wouldn't say I was jealous, I don't think I'm a jealous person,' said FA Cup winner Angie Poppy, 'but I'm envious of the footballers now, with their facilities, their training, their coaching, playing full-time, getting a wage, and the places they travel – I travelled to places with the England team, but my goodness, they've been all over the world if they're fortunate enough to play for England now or one of the big clubs.'

Her former team-mate Vicky Johnson was delighted that modern players had so many opportunities – but thought things could improve further. 'It's come a long way, and I'm so happy and glad that girls today have got the opportunity to be affiliated to a club and they have all the facilities, and it's getting more and more coverage,' she said. 'It just needs to be on par a bit more with the men's [game] really.'

Carol Parry, the closest relative of England's first official goalscorer Sylvia Gore, thought that her cousin would have continued to support today's players. 'If she was still alive today I think she'd find how wonderful it had become, how it speeded up, women's football, with the World Cup, and I think she would have been in her element to think how well it has been supported, really. I think she was obviously trying a long time in her early career to get women's football off the ground and recognised that they're just as good as the men. I think she would have been really pleased, the way it's gone.'

'Of course I think it's hard for any athlete of any generation that has achieved something, teams or individually, to sometimes feel like you've not necessarily got the acknowledgement you feel the team warrants or deserves or the club warrants for what it's achieved,' reflected Anita Asante, at that time still playing for Aston Villa at the highest level, and who some months later announced her retirement from football at the end of the 2021/22 season. 'And we know that's not because of us. That's because everyone else has been too slow to join in and support the game and watch the games and take interest in teams and players. I think collectively the memories hold strong for us and we are all obviously really proud of that.

'But, yes, of course, it's a shame that the lack of archiving of the women's game can diminish the magnitude of what has been achieved – whether it be us or even before us to the point where we have been able to do what we did then.'

Karen Farley loved to watch the current generation of England players. She enthused about Lucy Bronze's stunning goal against Norway in the 2015 Women's World Cup, and was so pleased that fans now could watch England compete at the highest level.

'It's so fantastic that these kids can now see that – "I can be that". We didn't have those when we were kids – we didn't have any [female] role models. My role models were Kenny Dalglish and Graeme Souness and all of these. So, yeah, it is fantastic where we are today, and I feel very privileged to have had the chance to do what I did, and to experience what I had.'

It was a sharp contrast to her memories of England's first Women's World Cup campaign, back in 1995. The only TV coverage she could remember was a ten-minute highlights package.

'It was quite patronising, the way they were talking about us – it was almost like, "Look at them, bless them, look how well they're doing,"' she said. She remembered Channel 4's coverage of the Women's FA Cup, which petered out before the turn of the millennium, and removed the one consistent annual showcase for women's football on national television. Even so, she was sure girls growing up in the 1990s and later had things easier than those playing a decade or two or three before.

'When I read all these interviews with the stars of today, and they're like, "Oh, we had such a struggle when we were young, there was nothing," I'm like, "Hold on a second, love." You had a struggle? Because I wasn't allowed to play football at school. I was banned from playing football in school, because I was a girl.'

When England played Germany at Wembley in November 2019, former players were invited to the game, and did a lap of honour around the pitch at half-time – some recognition for the years in which their own matches were ignored, dismissed or unreported.

Farley was there, with her partner, and was unimpressed with the way that some of today's players behaved, rejecting requests for autographs. 'When fame and fortune comes in, don't forget. We were the ones that made it, made you able to be what you are today. We were the ones that put up with all of the crap – the name-calling, the ridicule, the amount of times that people would just say, "You reckon you can play football? Yeah, right, love, you're a girl, don't be so ridiculous." But I'm old-school and I'm of that era that if someone comes up to you and wants to talk to you about what you're doing, you do it. You take those five minutes – or 30 seconds to sign an autograph book.'

Former captain Faye White was also there, with her young sons sitting in the stands. Although she had told them many times about her footballing career, it was then that her achievements seemed to sink in.

'When there's a game on the telly, I'll say, "I used to play there" – some of the Premiership grounds,' she said. 'You think, "Wow, so many other footballers would have loved those opportunities."'

Her older son had taken some of her medals into school to show his classmates, and one of his friends had spotted a photo of White when he went on a tour of the Arsenal stadium.

'He asked, "Mummy, are you famous?" And it's like, "No, not really. I used to play football."'

AFTERWORD

FINALLY – AFTER SO LONG – ENGLAND had a major international football trophy to celebrate. The Lionesses, like Sir Alf Ramsey's men of 1966, beat Germany at Wembley after extra-time to claim their title at the climax of the UEFA Women's EURO 2022. Amidst delirious scenes, Sarina Wiegman's women were crowned champions of Europe, having defeated their old rivals 2–1 in front of 87,192 fans at the national stadium.

It was a summer like never before. There were footballers on the front and back pages of all the newspapers, and huge tabloid headlines cheering the national side on and urging the country to stop everything to watch. Radio and television talk shows alike were asking: 'Could this be the summer that England finally win?' Sure, the words might have sounded familiar, but this time it was the female footballers who had captured the hearts and imaginations of fans everywhere.

When Chloe Kelly scrambled the ball over the line and whipped off her shirt to whirl it around her head in sheer ecstasy – pausing briefly, of course, to check that no late flag from any assistant referee was about to wreck her dream – it was for many not just an iconic image but a turning point in history. It was the moment that women's football in England stepped up to the biggest stage of all.

In the minutes and hours immediately after such a famous win, very few people were thinking of how the Lionesses had made history, or how they had changed the game forever. The mood was simply one of celebration. Captain Leah Williamson hoisted the trophy aloft, and the entire squad cheered and cavorted on the pop-up podium as the confetti rained down on their heads.

'We talk and we talk and we talk, and we've finally done it!' an exuberantly tearful Williamson told the TV cameras, apparently referring to the incessant speculation before, during and after every senior international tournament as to when the glory of 1966 would finally be recreated.

Striker Ellen White – who would announce her retirement from all forms of football just a few days later – wrapped herself in a St George's flag, beaming but looking also slightly incredulous, perhaps struggling to believe that at the age of 33, after playing in three Women's World Cups, three Women's Euros, two Olympics and breaking the women's goalscoring record, she finally had a gold medal to treasure. Photographers snapped several of the players each taking a moment to have a quick sit-down and simply look adoringly at the medal hanging from her neck.

Sarina Wiegman might have expected that her post-match press conference might have been a pleasant but more sedate affair than the party on the pitch. But her players had very different ideas as they congaed into the room, singing the famous chorus of Three Lions – 'Football's coming home!' Goalkeeper Mary Earps leapt on to the desk to dance in front of her coach, Lucy Bronze beside her, before both jumped off and rejoined the merry throng. A laughing Wiegman looked on happily.

It was an only marginally more subdued squad – albeit with several wearing sunglasses, all the better to hide the after-effects of their celebrations the previous night – that bounced onto the stage at the Trafalgar Square fan zone the day afterwards. People had headed to one of London's most well-known public spaces to watch matches throughout the tournament; now they went there to acclaim the women who had won it. The personalities of the Lionesses shone through in what must have been a hastily-put-together public appearance, with veteran Jill Scott providing some surreal comedy as she began to interview the trophy, and best friends Millie Bright and Rachel Daly giving some indication of what a night out clubbing with them must be like as they led a lip-sync rendition of 'River Deep, Mountain High'.

There was space for only 7,000 spectators in Trafalgar Square that Monday, but millions across the country watched the clips on social media or television. So many times, English sports teams are praised for their effort, for their performance, and often for coming very close but failing to triumph. This day, however, was one to mark a victory, and as people all over England shared the videos and the links to articles, they also shared the Lionesses' joy.

Even writing these words, looking at the photos and watching the video footage makes me teary. For me – and for thousands of others watching – England's win was not just about one match, or one tournament. It was everything.

BBC presenter Gabby Logan signed off after the final with a nod back to the boys of 1966 and Kenneth Wolstenholme's legendary commentary. 'They think it's all over? It's only just begun.' She was highlighting the fact that a trophy win of such magnitude guaranteed only bigger and better things for the Lionesses and the generations to follow. No more would the game skulk in the shadows of the achievements of their male counterparts.

In such a wave of excitement and emotion, it was easy to overlook the fact that, of course, 2022 by no means marked the start of women's football in England. One person who was keen to ensure that nobody mistakenly thought that was Sarina Wiegman herself, who was pressed for comment time and again by reporters wanting to revel in football finally 'coming home'. Always thoughtful, often reserved, the Dutchwoman is famous among journalists for refusing to be drawn on commenting on individual players, preferring to focus on the result and the contribution from the team as a whole. What Wiegman likes is perspective and context.

One thing she said that summer that really stood out to me was this: 'We should always remember the ones who went before us because they really made a path for us.'

She had been at pains prior to and throughout the campaign to recognise the achievements of the women who had laid the foundations for her squad of full-time professionals to excel. Women who had been scorned and mocked for their love of the beautiful game. Women who had spent their limited leave from work travelling round the world to represent their country. Women who had been banned from playing on a football pitch at all.

The Lionesses of the past had hardly been lionised. Their achievements had not been widely reported, and on the rare occasions that they had received media attention they were trivialised or demeaned simply for being women. And before an official England team had even been permitted, there were women who defied societal expectations, who laughed at the idea that they should be prevented from kicking a ball just as their brothers did. Some played under pseudonyms; others – as is the case for so many women throughout history – left limited documentation behind them, meaning their personal stories are next to impossible to piece together. But all of them were pioneers.

I was impressed by Wiegman's public acknowledgement that there were decades of women's football that had been overlooked, rather than pretending it was something new. At last there was a discussion about the way the authorities had attempted to crush it, and how belittling attitudes persist even now. And where Wiegman led, her players followed, making sure they gave credit wherever possible to the generations that had gone before them – the ones who had laid the groundwork and fought so many battles to enable a top-class squad of full-time professional female footballers to live out their wildest dreams.

In 2022 the Lionesses' camp opened its arms to the women who had laid a path for them. Long-retired players were invited to training sessions. Those who had never before received a proper international cap were finally presented with one by veteran Jill Scott and Euros-winning captain Leah Williamson during a ceremony hosted in the Wembley dressing rooms ahead of England's autumn friendly against world champions the USA. An honour roll of former players was invited to take a walk round the pitch in front of a sell-out crowd, finally receiving the public acclaim that had eluded them during their own days as Lionesses.

During the golden summer and reflective autumn of 2022, several former Lionesses found themselves in the mainstream media spotlight for more or less the first time: first official skipper Sheila Parker, smiling and waving from a wheelchair after a spell of ill health; Carol Thomas, who had worn the armband in England's first European final in 1984, suddenly a much-sought-after interviewee; and Gill Coultard, whose long career stretched over three decades. All three tell their stories in this book, amongst a clutch of other inspirational and previously ignored women.

Unsuitable for Females takes its name from the words of a now-notorious FA memo outlawing women's football on affiliated pitches. It tells the story of the women of whom Wiegman spoke – those who played after the ban was lifted wearing the shirt of their country for the sheer honour of it, but also those who played in spite of the rule telling them not to. It is both a snapshot of history and a thank-you to the women who fought and blazed a trail for future generations.

How reassuring it is to know that today's Lionesses understand that. And that they continue to campaign for the women who will follow them. Almost before the Wembley confetti settled, they released an open letter calling on politicians to commit to providing girls with the same opportunities to play football as their male counterparts. It is heartening and thrilling to hear Sarina Wiegman say that her team know they stand in their predecessors' debt – and that they owe a duty to those who will follow them. As she added: 'This team makes a path for the next generation.'

REFERENCES

Bolton, Steve (2020), 'Molly Seaton – Ireland's Best': https://www.playingpasts.co.uk/

Bolton, Steve (2020), 'Lily Parr – Amateur Cricketer, Hockey Player, Footballer': https://www.playingpasts.co.uk/

Bolton, Steve (2020), 'Football and the Great Game': https://www.wlv.ac.uk/research/institutes-and-centres/centre-for-historical-research/football-and-war-network/football-and-war-blog/2020/football-and-the-great-gameworld-war-one-some-remarkable-images/

Bolton, Steve (2021), 'The Pioneering Manchester Ladies: Part One': https://gjfootballarchive.com/

Brennan, Patrick, 'The British Ladies' Football Club': http://www.donmouth.co.uk/

Brennan, Patrick, 'Nettie Honeyball': http://www.donmouth.co.uk/

Cunningham, Sam (2021), 'Patricia Gregory: We never imagined girls would be paid to play football': https://inews.co.uk/

Davies, Pete (1997), *I Lost My Heart to the Belles*

Day, Dave and Margaret Roberts (2019), 'From Butlins to Europe: Fodens Ladies in the 1960s and 1970s', *Sport in History* 39:4, 418–44

Dunn, Carrie and Joanna Welford (2014), *Football and the FA Women's Super League*

Jenkel, Lisa (2020): 'The FA's Ban of Women's Football 1921 in the Contemporary Press: A Historical Discourse Analysis', *Sport in History*, Vol. 41, Issue 2

Lee, James, 'The Lady Footballers and the British Press, Critical Survey Vol. 24', No. 1, *Sporting Victorians* (2012), pp. 88–101

Newsham, Gail (2018), *In a League of Their Own! The Dick, Kerr Ladies 1917–1965*

Lopez, Sue (1997), *Women on the Ball: A Guide to Women's Football*

Owen, Wendy (2005), *Kicking Against Tradition: A Career in Women's Football*

Williams, Jean (2003), *A Game for Rough Girls? A History of Women's Football in Britain*

Williamson, David (1991), *Belles of the Ball*

Wilson, Jeremy (2020), 'How super striker Sue Lopez paved way for the professionals', *The Daily Telegraph*, 24 April 2020

ACKNOWLEDGEMENTS

AS ALWAYS, THERE ARE A lot of people I need to thank for their hundreds of kindnesses as I have written this book.

Thank you to all the former players and administrators who have spoken to me for this book, on and off the record; it has been an honour and a privilege. Thank you for trusting me, for sharing your stories with me, for the emails and photographs, for the texts and WhatsApp messages to fill in the blanks.

Getting hold of academic material when you are outside academia – and even when you're inside it – can sometimes be tricky. Thank you so much to Dr Ali Bowes for her help accessing resources. Thank you to Dr Fiona Skillen for fascinating and useful background information on women's leisure activities in the early part of the 20th century. Professor Jean Williams is as always an absolute treasure trove of unsurpassed insight into the history of the women's game, and Gail Newsham's expertise on the subject of the Dick, Kerr Ladies is both unparalleled and stunning – what a life's work. Thank you to Stephen Bolton for his research and also his personal memories, and thank you to Stuart Gibbs and Andy Mitchell for sharing their own discoveries and theories; Patrick Brennan's online collection of archive materials from the early years of women's football was incredibly valuable. It was lovely to catch up with Carol Parry; it was a delight to get to know her cousin Sylvia Gore in the last years of her life and wonderful to find out more about her younger years.

I'm indebted to Karen Falconer and Carol West of the FA Women's National League for their assistance in tracking down players. Thank you to Chris Slegg for his guidance on the topic of the Women's FA Cup, to Nicole Allison for her help, and to David Williamson for his assistance and generosity on the topic of the British Ladies' Football Club. Thank you to Ali Rampling for her brilliant feature on Lowestoft Ladies and for putting me in touch with so many of the leading lights. Thank you to my friend and previous collaborator Dr Jo Welford; it was lovely to have a chat and to explore just how women's football has changed in the years since, in our incarnations as academics, we assessed the launch of the Women's Super League.

Thanks again to Gail Newsham for the incredible photo of Dick, Kerr Ladies that appears on the cover of this book, and to Girls on the Ball for the photo of the Lionesses in action. Thanks, of course, to Alison Rae and Neville Moir at Arena for their patience and wise counsel.

Thank you to the highly esteemed figures in sports media for their kind words about me and my work that I've been privileged to be able to use on the cover of this book.

And as always, thank you to Julian for looking after our rescue dog Spring and taking on the responsibility of the new house renovations, housework, plus of course the hot beverage provision while I finished the manuscript. Put the kettle on.

INDEX